INDEPENDENTS
RISING

ALSO BY JACQUELINE S. SALIT

Talk/Talk: Making (Non) Sense of an Irrational World

INDEPENDENTS
RISING

OUTSIDER MOVEMENTS,
THIRD PARTIES,
AND THE STRUGGLE FOR
A POST-PARTISAN AMERICA

JACQUELINE S. SALIT

First published in 2012 by PALGRAVE MACMILLAN® in the United States—a division of St. Martin's Press LLC, 175 Fifth Avenue, New York, NY 10010.

Where this book is distributed in the UK, Europe and the rest of the world, this is by Palgrave Macmillan, a division of Macmillan Publishers Limited, registered in England, company number 785998, of Houndmills, Basingstoke, Hampshire RG21 6XS.

Palgrave Macmillan is the global academic imprint of the above companies and has companies and representatives throughout the world.

Palgrave® and Macmillan® are registered trademarks in the United States, the United Kingdom, Europe and other countries.

ISBN: 978-0-230-33912-5

Library of Congress Cataloging-in-Publication Data
Salit, Jacqueline.
    Independents rising : outsider movements, third parties, and the struggle for a post-partisan America / by Jacqueline Salit.
        p.   cm.
    Includes bibliographical references and index.
    ISBN 978-0-230-33912-5 (hardback)
    1. Party affiliation—United States. 2. Political parties—United States. 3. Third parties (United States politics) 4. United States—Politics and government. I. Title.
JK2271.S25   2012
324.273—dc23

                                                                        2011052877

A catalogue record of the book is available from the British Library.

Design by Letra Libre Inc.

First edition: August 2012

10 9 8 7 6 5 4 3 2 1

Printed in the United States of America.

CONTENTS

For Sema,

fiercely independent

PREFACE

WHEN I PUT TOGETHER THE OUTLINE FOR THIS BOOK IN THE SPRING OF 2011, IT was offered to a number of publishers. The first response was a rejection. The editors liked the timing and the topic of the book and thought I was qualified to write it. But they balked at the notion that my story was based on my personal experiences, rather than dictated by a single illuminating and unifying idea.

My agent, Robert Guinsler, asked me what I thought. I told him I was guilty as charged.

I began my political life in New York City while still a child. In my house, politics is what we did, instead of going on family camping trips or to Disneyland. (We actually did go to Disneyland, once, in 1967.) Eugene McCarthy volunteers slept in our living room for three months in 1968. My father, who had an advertising agency (it wasn't like *Mad Men*—this was the Jewish and Italian side of the business), wrote ad copy for antiwar and reform candidates. My mother took us to freedom school and to march on Washington. My younger sister, at age 12, started an alternative high school. I mainly volunteered for Democratic candidates, but I also worked for Republican John Lindsay in 1965. (The guys were cuter.) For the first half of the 1970s, I worked in the news division of one of the then-three major networks. Politics and propaganda were in my blood.

By the mid-1970s, the social and cultural upheavals of the 1960s were over. My mother, sister, and I became part of a tightly knit circle of progressive innovators led by a genius tactician and radical postmodern entrepreneur, Fred Newman, who foresaw the market for a new genre of humanist psychology and independent post-partisan politics. Newman was an extraordinary, though not capricious, risk taker. In 1979, when independent politics was as unknown as a starting contestant on *American Idol,* he launched the New Alliance Party (NAP). At that time, 57 percent of high school students believed that a third party was illegal. Being an independent—rather than a Democrat or Republican—was roughly the equivalent of being a nudist. You had the right to be one—this is America, after all!—but everyone would appreciate it if you kept it to yourself.

The New Alliance Party was very successful for a left-wing third party. It ran candidates for public office in the Democratic primaries and, win or lose, as independents in the general election. The tactic became known as "inside/outside" and caused quite a stir. It was especially embraced in the black, Latino, gay, and progressive white communities in New York City and was a refuge for Democratic elected officials of color who had been shafted by their own party and took to using independent politics to punish their tormentors. As the NAP expanded nationally, it was also a kind of incubator for a new generation of activists who organized around the need to expand American democracy rather than focusing on traditional issues; they were "process progressives." The NAP's 1988 presidential candidate, Lenora Fulani, became the first African American and first woman in U.S. history to achieve access to the ballot in all 50 states. Later, the NAP joined forces with the Perot movement in a startling left/right, black/white coalition for political reform.

The New Alliance Party was deeply disliked by the Official Left, which focused exclusively on its interminable quest to control the Democratic Party. For them, independent politics was an idea whose time had definitely *not* come! (They weren't crazy about a new psychology either, no pun intended.) The tensions between the independent progressives and the Democrat-aligned progressives were very heated during the 1980s and 1990s, eventually reaching all the way to the White House. I came of age, politically speaking, in that surprisingly bitter crucible.

With the arrival of Ross Perot, the independent movement exploded, almost overnight. Jesse Ventura. Ralph Nader. Michael Bloomberg. Thirty-five percent of Americans said they were independents. A paradigm shift was underway, and I was smack in the middle of it all. I was a player in the right/left politics of the national Reform Party. In New York City, I served as manager for all three Bloomberg mayoral campaigns on the Independence Party line, in 2001, 2005, and 2009. Today, I am the president of

IndependentVoting.org, the progressive wing of the independent movement that leads active groups of grassroots independent voters in nearly every state. If my personal career is at all notable, it is simply because the improbable came to pass: Independent voters are now driving American politics. Being an independent is no longer esoteric or fringe. It's as American as apple pie.

Back to my guilty plea. This book was written from my personal experiences. It's not an academic narrative. It's not "the whole story." I've tried to give an honest and unvarnished account of events, personalities, and contexts in the formative decades of what I feel certain will turn out to be a century-defining dynamic.

The independent political movement has an actual history. The 40 percent of Americans who identify as independents have an actual history. They are not an invention of recent years, nor are they just an "idea," unified, illuminating, or otherwise. Like all other social movements, this one has been shaped by events and conflicts that stretch over several decades. I was there for many of them. I wanted to write this book because independents are all too frequently treated by pundits and politicians alike as an idea—at best, these days, as "an idea whose time has come." But, still, an idea. Nothing could be further from the truth.

When a fringe movement crosses over into the political mainstream, as this one has, it faces new challenges and choices. I hope that this book contributes to a healthy and vigorous debate within the independent movement and with its allies on what to do next. Frankly, I also hope the book pisses off some people. Hurtful things have been done to independents in the name of "progressivism." I'd like to think there will be no more of that, but it's doubtful.

Finally, I hope this book helps people to see how emerging movements, not unlike emerging markets, need to be nurtured and developed, even when there is no predictable outcome attached to their growth. Doing so raises complex and exciting political, legal, cultural, financial, and tactical questions. New thinking and doing are urgently needed to answer them.

Independents are rising. They are rising to the challenge of remaking American democracy. This is their story.

INDEPENDENTS
RISING

INTRODUCTION

IN POLITICS, AS IN HISTORY, IT SOMETIMES PAYS TO BE A LITERALIST.

I believe that if you take things at face value, you will often discover important truths that analysts and casual perusers skip over. That's in large part the key to grasping what's happening with independent voters today.

Suddenly, there's much ado about independents. No one put it more succinctly than the respected pollster Charlie Cook in March 2011: "Independent voters are the ones who matter most in American politics."[1] Forty percent of Americans today identify as independents, the highest proportion in 70 years. Naturally, they raise plenty of questions. Are they left or right? Liberal or conservative? In the middle? Angry or merely frustrated? Pro- or anti-government? A base for a third party? Inclined to vote Democrat or Republican? After all, independents voted for Barack Obama, a Democrat, in 2008, and then, in a seeming 180-degree reversal, for Republican congressional candidates in 2010. Who are these independents? A profusion of polling, focus groups, and profiles are suddenly dedicated to answering that very question.

This is where the literal reading comes in handy. As someone involved in organizing independents for 30 years, I would advise putting all of the "data" to one side. Listen to the simplest, the most obvious statement independents are making. No interpretation, polling, or focus group is needed.

They are Americans who don't want to align with any political party.

In a culture that is so overwhelmingly defined by and permeated with the politics of parties (especially the big two), it's remarkable that so many Americans choose to define themselves otherwise. In many cases, doing so means they forfeit some basic rights, such as voting in a primary. But they do it anyway.

That independent voters have become, as Charlie Cook says, "the ones who matter most in American politics" took plenty of folks by surprise, including Cook. Some years back he and I ran into each other at a private meeting of political consultants in Washington. I was briefing the group on the emergence of the independent voter as a new and combustible force. He told me that there was no such thing as an independent, only voters who "leaned" or were late deciders for one of the two parties. Things got pretty heated. Afterward, he apologized and said he hoped he hadn't been rude. I accepted his apology, explaining that he wasn't rude, just wrong! Suffice it to say, I was happy to read the above quote, at long last.

An independent realignment has been taking shape, in fits and starts, for more than 20 years. And within that realignment—or, as some call it, disalignment—an organized independent movement has taken shape. For a decade it was largely, though not exclusively, a third-party movement. After 2000, it moved in a more disparate, even anti-party direction. Instead of being a party-building movement, it became a fusion movement (more on that distinction later).

Its prehistory dates back to the John Anderson campaign of 1980, when Anderson, a liberal Republican congressman from Illinois, broke ranks with his party, ran for president as an independent, and garnered 7 percent of the vote. Though his candidacy created the national Unity Party, it went out of business when he endorsed Democrat Walter Mondale for president in 1984. Anderson remained an active champion of nonpartisan political reform.

But if Anderson was a political "one-hit wonder," in 1988 two very different independent presidential candidates gained a toehold that would launch significant political careers. Lenora Fulani, a developmental psychologist, ran for president as the candidate of the New Alliance Party and broke through a glass ceiling when she accessed the ballot in all 50 states, becoming the first ever woman and first African American to do so. Fulani would go on to create a controversial left/right coalition with Perot voters after 1992 that led to the formation of the national Reform Party in 1996, which backed Perot's second run. Fulani remained a major force in the Reform Party until its virtual demise in 2000. She also became a key player in the New York City Independence Party, which helped elect Mayor Michael Bloomberg in 2001 and drew 47 percent of black voters away from the Democratic Party to vote for

Bloomberg in 2005. Today Fulani is considered the country's leading black political independent.

Also in 1988, Ron Paul, at the time a little-known physician and standard-bearer of the Libertarian Party, polled a half million votes in his independent presidential bid. Later elected to Congress as a Republican from Texas, Paul ran in the 2008 Republican primary for president, startling party hierarchs with the strength of his support from libertarian Republicans and independents who voted in open GOP primaries and caucuses. His bid spawned the Campaign for Liberty, which helped propel his son Rand Paul's successful Tea Party–backed campaign for the U.S. Senate from Kentucky in 2010. Ron Paul reprised his role as an antiestablishment contender in the Republican contest for the 2012 presidential nomination, mobilizing a strong showing from independents in open contests and striving to become a power broker in the GOP.

But if Anderson, Fulani, and Paul were independent canaries in the political coal mine, Ross Perot ignited the explosion that shook the party system to its bedrock. For all of Perot's peculiar pronouncements and folksy but autocratic style, he opened a window on a subterranean disgust with the corruption and partisanship of government that mainstream politicians had long ignored. At one point he was polling at 42 percent, and America was poised to send an independent to the White House. Then, in the summer of 1992, he mysteriously suspended his campaign, flew to New York City (the site of the Democratic Convention), and announced his withdrawal from the race, declaring that the Democratic Party had been rehabilitated. He got back into the race in August, leveraged his way into the televised presidential debates, and polled 19 percent of the vote.

Perot's blend of political reform, populism, economic nationalism, and fiscal conservatism struck a chord for many Americans. Once his 19 million votes had been counted, Democrats and Republicans wasted no time trying to make inroads into this energized independent constituency. The Democratic Leadership Council, which provided the political framing for Bill Clinton's centrist New Democrat approach, began a major study of the Perot voter in an effort to chart a pathway to a future coalition. In 1994, Newt Gingrich's Contract with America borrowed components of the Perot movement's political and fiscal agenda, including plans to reform Congress and balance the budget, and rode its populist message to Republican control of the House.

The major parties tried to retrofit themselves to engage and co-opt the Perot movement (while holding on to their partisan cores). But it was developing a life of its own, which included the short-lived Patriot Party—a precursor and catalyst for the national Reform Party. This new political theater created a set of original dramas (and a few comedies) in which major players from both sides of the aisle attempted to intervene.

Former Colorado Governor Richard Lamm, a Democrat, unsuccessfully challenged Perot for the Reform Party nomination in 1996, in what many saw as an attempted takeover of the new party by a circle of centrist, mainly Democratic, politicians.[2]

After Perot's second run in 1996 and the election of independent Jesse Ventura as governor of Minnesota in 1998, the Reform coalition was an uneasy one. This broke into open confrontation in 1999. The Ventura wing and the Fulani wing joined together to elect a new party chairman opposed to Perot, part of an effort to move the Reform Party beyond the limits of its founder. This revolt sparked a counterrevolution by Dallas Perot loyalists, which spurred the 2000 bid by conservative Republican commentator Pat Buchanan for the party's presidential nomination. His effort to turn Reform into a social conservative party failed. But this battle, combined with the controversy surrounding Ralph Nader's 2000 presidential run on the Green Party ticket, sent the national third-party movement into hibernation.

Nader's campaign, which polled 2.75 percent of the vote, fell short of the Green Party's aim to gain recognition as a national party, for which 5 percent of the vote for president is needed. Nader's effort to use independent politics to pull the Democratic Party to the left was overshadowed by the accusation that he had cost Al Gore the election and put George W. Bush in the White House, making Nader the scourge of the liberal intelligentsia. Nader ran again in 2004, without the support of the Green Party or the left glitterati, but with the support of the Fulani forces and the remnants of the Reform Party, to no great impact. Meanwhile, Ron Paul's shift out of third-party politics and into the Republican fold helped to marginalize the Libertarian Party and drew Paul's followers into the GOP.

For all intents and purposes, the national third-party move-ment was on life support. The Reform Party's attempt to be a non-ideological party of political and economic reform was busted. And the ideological third parties found themselves at odds with emerging changes in the electorate. In 2000, the year the third-party movement effectively died, 35 percent of Americans were in-dependents. By 2006, independents were inaugurating a political swing era. Independent politics was no longer about a third party. It was an agitated rejection of partisanship, leading to unpredict-able voting patterns that expressed that rejection.

After the implosion of the Perot movement in 2000, indepen-dent voters spent several national election cycles evenly dividing their votes between Democratic and Republican candidates for president and Congress. In the 2006 midterms, however, a ma-jor shift occurred, when 59 percent of independents—frustrated with the Bush administration and its prosecution of the war in Iraq—voted for Democratic House candidates, ending a 12-year run of Republican control of Congress.[3] But the full effect of the antiestablishment impulse among independents (then 36 per-cent of the electorate) was most keenly felt in the dramatic 2008 competition between Barack Obama and Hillary Clinton for the Democratic Party's presidential nomination. In the 33 states where independents were permitted to vote in the presidential primaries and caucuses, 65 percent of those participating chose to vote on the Democratic side, and nearly 60 percent of them cast ballots for Obama.[4] A close examination of the numbers reveals that if those contests had been limited to Democrats, Hillary Clinton would have been the party's nominee.

Obama went on to beat Republican John McCain with an eight-point margin among independents[5]—ironically, since McCain owed his own candidacy to the support of independents who had chosen GOP ballots and him during the crucial early primaries, notably New Hampshire's.[6] Thus, in 2008 independents upended the Democratic Party establishment by backing Obama, made the maverick McCain viable, and then chose the winner in the November general election.

Their impact only intensified in the 2010 midterms when 59 percent of independents swung against the party in power, handing the GOP majority control of the House and the president a divided legislature.[7] This liberated Obama from the partisanship of his own political party, but it also empowered the Tea Party, which gained notoriety just months after Obama took office. Though some pegged the Tea Party as an independent movement, it was immediately absorbed into the Republican Party, converting its economic populism into fiscal and social conservatism.

A MISUNDERSTOOD MOVEMENT

Yet, as important as independent voters have become, they are only vaguely understood and almost always analyzed through the prism of parties. Though political parties are never once mentioned in the Constitution, they have evolved into quasi-governmental institutions with sweeping powers. Nonetheless, being in a party is actually rejected by four in ten Americans. Incredibly, some analysts still echo the old Charlie Cook argument that there aren't many "true" independents, because most tend to vote for Republicans or Democrats in the end anyway.

This kind of parochialism runs so deep that the commentariat barely recognizes this massive disalignment as a critique of the two-party system. If 40 percent of America's children decided they wanted to move away from home, preferring to visit their parents only when they chose to, this would spark a national furor over the failures of parenting, along with a variety of measures, some coercive, to get those kids back into the house. But when 40 percent of adults resist putting their politics in partisan terms (which to many people is more important and less fleeting than who they vote for in a given election), it is not cause for any introspection. After all, the partisans reason, so long as the independents vote for us, who cares what they call themselves?

Not so fast. What you call yourself actually has meaning in American history. Our forebearers (twice or thrice removed for most of us) fought a revolution because Parliament's disregard for the colonists' self-rule pushed them to the point where they could no longer call themselves British, but had to instead call themselves Americans. The Boston Tea Partiers did not throw English tea into the harbor because of the tax. They weren't antitax social conservatives. English tea was actually cheaper than other teas, even with the tax. The revolutionists threw tea into the harbor because an alien government half a world away was promulgating laws without the consent of the governed. As historian Gordon Wood notes in *The Idea of America,* Americans were "a people caught up in a revolutionary situation, deeply alienated from the existing sources of authority and vehemently involved in a basic reconstruction of their political and social order."[8] It was about democracy and representation, not the price of tea.

Though in 2008 independents were permitted to vote in presidential primaries and caucuses in 33 states and made full use of that opportunity, elections for public office below the presidency are far more restricted. Only 25 states have laws permitting independents to vote in non-presidential primaries, and that permission is often dependent on the parties agreeing to accept nonaligned voters. Currently, there are efforts underway to roll back open primaries in states that have them. Independent voters are challenging that regression in court. This has given rise to a new set of constitutional controversies over party rights vs. voter rights. Efforts at nonpartisan reform of the closed systems have met with fierce hostility from the political parties—both major and, surprisingly, minor.

This book chronicles the rise of independent voters over the last 25 years, how the self-perpetuating culture of partisanship is choking the country, and how independent voters are rejecting the controlling authority of political parties. It explores how that conflict is assuming center stage in American politics (though it is not about restoring a "center"!), and it shares the bottom-up history of an independent movement that has grown in the midst of that conflict. I have been fortunate to have played a role in that story, and I can report some unseen and untold aspects of it.

Some might say that independents, the 40 percent of voters not fully integrated into the political system, are simply the next group of Americans to be unfairly excluded. In other words, independents' demand for equality should be seen as a classic civil rights issue. But there is a difference worth noting. The diverse interests that fought to win inclusion in political affairs and thus came to be represented by political parties were largely defined by existential factors. Black people did not choose to be black (not to mention slaves). Women were excluded because of their gender. The poor and workingmen and -women could not escape their economic and social status for most of history. These interests were defined by a combination of biology, economics, and fortune or misfortune.

Their integration into the political process was part of America's social and economic growth, as the expansion, distribution, and redistribution of the fruits of American labor and enterprise were continually negotiated. Political parties—including third parties— played a vigorous role in that. Fairness and economic strength were thought to be intrinsically intertwined. Today, the dominant parties seem incapable of synthesizing these things. And the structural partisanship they have engineered forms, if anything, an insurmountable obstacle to progress.

Independents, while a vast *underrepresented* community of Americans, are not a political class that forms as a matter of destiny. They have *chosen* this identity, and thereby made a small but distinct declaration of noncompliance. Arguably, they are a social engine for political reform that goes beyond parties, partisanship, and traditional ideology. In this respect, independents are, by their choice, radicals—nonideological radicals, but radicals just the same.

Mistaken assumptions about independents abound. The most persistent, of course, is that independents are neither liberal nor conservative, but "in the middle," ergo moderates or centrists. On the one hand, this "insight" derives from polls, which often show independents to the left of most Republicans and to the right of most Democrats on a set of hot-button issues. This is often used as evidence that independents are at the center; a statement increasingly proven false. In May 2011, the Pew Research Center released its latest political typology report, "Beyond Red vs. Blue," asserting that independents are not moderates but, instead, span the spectrum and combine social and economic views in unorthodox ways. Indeed, independents are responding much more to the power gap between political elites at the top and ordinary Americans at the bottom than whatever space exists between the right and the left. The emerging independent movement is regularly convulsed by political conflicts over this issue—populism vs. centrism.

The centrist paradigm is itself filled with ambiguities. Exactly what does "in the middle" mean? Is it an emotional or ideological space? If you married and divorced twice, are you "in the middle" of spouse number one and spouse number two? I don't think so. Arguably (even if not emotionally), you have moved on. If you grew up drinking orange juice, then switched to grapefruit juice

in college, but in your thirties decided to stop drinking citrus altogether because the acid bothered your stomach, no one would
reasonably call you "in the middle" between orange juice and
grapefruit juice. And that would be true even if you drank orange
juice or grapefruit juice from time to time because the store had
run out of everything else.

The problem with this "middle" or "centrist" construct is that
it defines independents entirely in relation to the political parties
and their accompanying ideologies. Yet, this is the very institutional framing that independents are opting out of. The establishment fervor for the centrist label looks like a way of shoehorning
independents back into a partisan and ideological fold. This conflict has shaped the independent movement from its earliest days.

But, wherever independents are on the standard horizontal
spectrum, they are in the crosshairs when it comes to acting as
political change agents. As battle-hardened New York political
observer Doug Muzzio once remarked, "He who determines the
rules, rules."[9] In my experience, independents well understand that
political fact of life, and they see changing the *process* of politics as
fundamental to moving forward on public policy and developing
American culture and enterprise. That's been a premise of the independent movement, from its prehistory to the Perot explosion,
to contemporary independents' push for a postpartisan America.

The voting patterns of independents, past and future, are best
understood in relationship to their concerns about the partisanship of the political process. When independents gave Obama

the presidency, they wanted a postpartisan president. They had not and did not become Democrats. When, two years later, they wrested control of the House from Democrats and gave it to the GOP, it was because the nonpartisanship they wanted had not been realized. They had not become Republicans. Indeed, the post-midterm election Gallup polls showed the percentage of independents increasing (38 percent), the percentage of Democrats on a decline (31 percent), and Republican levels virtually static (29 percent).[10]

The story of the antiestablishment energy and influence of independent voters is compelling and largely untold. The independent movement and the mass defection from the parties are not equivalent. The movement is small, more organized, and more tactical, though it lives within and leads—in complex ways—the broad and volatile cross-section of Americans who are defying categories and categorization. The movement has been struggling to define itself from the shock wave of the Perot movement of the 1990s to the antipartisan electoral swings of the 2000s. Some of the names associated with that history are famous. Some of the movement's most important players you've never heard of until now. You will meet them in this book. And you will see them interacting with, influencing, challenging, frustrating, and in some cases prevailing over the big name players. They are as much the propellants of this movement as the headliners.

Independents are rising. We are at the start of an independent century. Literally.

ONE

1992

A YEAR OF AWKWARD CONTRADICTIONS

History shows that the group which successfully responds to one challenge is rarely the successful respondent to the next. . . . Those who have succeeded once are apt, in the next occasion, to be found "resting on their oars."

—Arnold Toynbee[1]

POLITICAL REFORM WAS NOT A POPULAR ISSUE IN THE EARLY 1990S AMONG LIBERAL opinion makers. Nor was it popular with the major political parties. Both were already struggling to redefine, not reform, themselves in the era of globalization.

New economic realities were at center stage and they would soon upend longstanding political norms. As William Greider wrote in *One World, Ready or Not: The Manic Logic of Global Capitalism,* "The steady globalization of U.S. firms has created awkward contradictions and tangled national identities."[2]

For the Democratic Party left, with its bedrock constituencies of labor and African Americans getting hammered by the changing economic environment of globalization, the idea that the party system itself needed structural reform was a nonstarter. They saw themselves as the firewall against the rise of a new vulture capitalism. Centrist Democrats, on the other hand, welcomed globalization, claiming it could ultimately benefit workers and the poor. In both cases, these Democrats were distinctly at odds with the reform populism simmering just below the surface.

At first the signs of voter rebellion were faint, easy to miss or to write off as merely localized. In 1990 voters in two states elected independents as governors. Walter Hickel in Alaska and Lowell Weicker in Connecticut were well-known Republicans, Hickel a former governor and Weicker a former U.S. senator. Internal battles in the Alaska and Connecticut Republican Parties over taxes and abortion drove both to run as independents.

Weicker later faced harsh criticism in independent circles for having abandoned A Connecticut Party (the political party his run created) while he and his associates vied for position in the national independent movement after Perot's success in 1992. But whatever Weicker's own political aspirations might have been, in 1990 voters were attracted to the idea that effective leadership could come from outside the two parties.[3]

That same year, a Colorado voter initiative to impose term limits on members of Congress passed with a spectacular 71 percent of the vote.[4] Massachusetts adopted a political reform measure—again by referendum—to open the ballot more fully to independent candidates and parties. Also in 1990, a pre-Perot underground spring broke through. An advertising campaign to "Throw the Hypocritical Rascals Out," conceived and funded by Florida-based financial planner Jack Gargan, drew over three hundred thousand responses and nearly one million dollars in contributions. (Nine years later Gargan would challenge the Perot inner circle for control of the Reform Party. But all of that was yet to come.)

These rumblings did not register on most political radars. The big story in 1990 was that the Democrats had controlled the House of Representatives since 1948 (and always would) and that the Republicans controlled the White House (and likely would for at least another six years). It seemed to many observers that the century would wrap up without any major surprises in American politics. In 1989 political science professor Francis Fukuyama wrote an influential essay for the *National Interest* magazine called "The End of History?"[5] Fukuyama projected that the collapse of communism heralded a new international order of liberal democracy and stability. America would be the world's beacon and breadwinner. The world would now follow suit.[6] Few saw beyond that ostensibly happy horizon.

Yet even if the number of democratic states were to increase worldwide, there were signs that American democracy was troubled. In June 1992 pollster Gordon Black and political theorist Theodore Lowi published the first major survey of voter discontent. Lowi, in his introduction to the survey, noted:

> There is a dirty little secret that sophisticates have been hiding from the masses for three or four decades. The secret is that the two-party system is dying . . . the two-party system has been kept alive with artificial respiration through state laws biased against third parties and through artificial insemination by federal subsidies and other protections sold to the public as "campaign reform." The two-party system would collapse in a moment if all the tubes and IVs were pulled out.[7]

The results of the survey indicated several remarkable trends. Dissatisfied voters were looking beyond traditional policy issues like taxes and the deficit and supporting extensive electoral reform. The crest of support for political reform was coming mainly from moderate and conservative voters.

Liberals and the left were hoping for the resurrection of liberalism, not the reform of two-partyism. Yet, voters were not keeping their antiestablishment impulses a secret. A term limits movement was gathering steam, prompting the founding of the group U.S. Term Limits in early 1992 by a coalition of libertarians and reform-minded Republicans. Hoping to reproduce the Colorado explosion, they collected the millions of signatures necessary to place referenda limiting members of Congress to two terms of office on the ballot in 13 states. The initiatives passed everywhere, regardless of "red" or "blue," with astonishing levels of support: Arizona 74 percent; Arkansas 60 percent; California 63 percent; Florida 77 percent; Michigan 59 percent; Missouri 74 percent; Montana 67 percent; North Dakota 55 percent; Ohio 66 percent; Oregon 69 percent; South Dakota 63 percent; Washington 52 percent; Wyoming 77 percent. A subterranean democracy revolt was breaking out into the open.[8] The liberal establishment was unmoved. As leading left commentators Alexander Cockburn and Andrew Kopkind observed in the *Nation*, "Liberals have become the most conservative element in American politics today where systemic change is involved."[9]

Then, a series of small but telling incidents early in the 1992 presidential campaign, not long before Ross Perot's electrifying announcement on *Larry King Live*, set the tone for the emerging friction between the pro-reform independent movement and the Democratic Party. It was January 1992 and candidate Bill Clinton was campaigning in New Hampshire, one of six top-tier contenders for the Democratic presidential nomination. Clinton was fending off a cascade of news stories about his sexual dalliances while trying to project his vision for a new, more centrist Democratic Party. There was also a seventh candidate—an independent, Lenora Fulani—who was beginning to present some problems for the granite state's Democratic Party.

A developmental psychologist and long-time progressive, born in Chester, Pennsylvania, and based in Harlem, Fulani had run for president as the candidate of the New Alliance Party in 1988, shattering a glass ceiling when she became the first African American and first female in U.S. history to achieve access to the presidential ballot in all 50 states. In 1992 Fulani entered the early Democratic primaries to promote her antipartisan pro-reform cause. She had been awarded nearly $650,000 in federal primary matching funds in December 1991. It's difficult to believe by today's standards, but Fulani's total of matchable dollars raised—heralded on the front page of the *New York Daily News* with the headline "The $642,000 Long Shot"—put her in second place among the top-tier Democrats, behind only Senator Tom Harkin, and $61,000 ahead of Bill Clinton.[10]

With a large campaign office on Elm Street, the main drag in Manchester, New Hampshire, a dozen full-time campaign staffers, and an aggressive message about reforming the party system, Fulani—a political outsider by virtually any measure—was making her presence felt. When the Democratic Party hosted a forum on health care in Nashua, Fulani and Larry Agran, the former mayor of Irvine, California, also a minor entrant in the presidential contest, forced their way onto the stage. Presidential hopeful and Virginia governor Douglas Wilder graciously conceded his time at the microphone to Fulani. Suddenly, the question of how the Democrats would deal with their "outsider" candidates became a public matter.

The chairman of the New Hampshire State Democratic Party (NHDP), Chris Spirou, wasted no time in laying down the law. He told the *Concord Monitor*, "Some of us in New Hampshire have

smelled the gunpowder of battle before. If they think they are going to intimidate Chris Spirou with these tactics, they are sadly
mistaken."[11]

By the time of the first televised debate, at WMUR's studios by
the Merrimack River in Manchester, the NHDP had taken pains to
block a repeat of Nashua. Pressured by Fulani's fund-raising prow-
ess, the executive director of the NHDP, Russell Verney, established new criteria for inclusion: Only those candidates who had
held statewide elective office would be eligible. (Ironically, Verney
would, in August, be recruited by Ross Perot to help steer his independent political aspirations. Verney and Fulani became sometimes allies and sometimes antagonists inside the Reform Party.)

The WMUR studios were locked behind a phalanx of
Manchester police on January 19, the night of the debate. Former
California governor Jerry Brown,[12] the progressive challenger to
the Clintonian Democratic Leadership Council (DLC) brand of
"new politics," issued a statement calling for Fulani's inclusion and
criticized the party for excluding her. "Our democratic system de-
mands a full and open process. Neither my campaign nor myself
will cooperate with efforts by the Democratic Party or other candidates to silence her voice."[13]

Fulani set up a mass picket ringing the studio, involving 400
protesters—some had traveled to New Hampshire from Harlem
but many were Manchester locals. The temperature that night was
a lip-splitting 12° F, but some protesters were gathered at both
entrances to the WMUR parking lot, taking turns warming up

inside heated buses. Television cameras and reporters clustered at the doorway to the studio. Jerry Brown arrived, stopping to shake hands with the picketers before entering. Not long afterward, a shiny black SUV pulled up at one of the entrances, attracting the attention of the crowd and the press. It slowed down to navigate the protesters. Bill Clinton was in the back seat. He and the car's other occupants were debating what to do. Suddenly Clinton dropped to the floor of the back seat, shielding his face from view as the car sped into the parking lot, past the police lines to the WMUR entrance.

The next day, Fred Newman, Fulani's political mentor and the architect of her candidacy, asked me to call the Clinton headquarters. I was deputy campaign manager and communications director, and our read on the episode at the studio entrance was that Clinton had felt a moment's hesitation about crossing the picket line and maybe even about the NHDP's ham-handed management of Fulani's exclusion. Apparently, we were at least partly right. The Clinton camp told me it wanted to avoid any future run-ins of this sort, which were an embarrassment to Clinton. Clinton campaign coordinator Mitchell Schwarz set up a meeting with Newman and me a few days later in the coffee shop at the Manchester Holiday Inn.

"What do you guys want?" Schwarz, young and brusque, asked as he arrived. We explained that our campaign was premised on the idea that independents wanted some very specific reforms of the political process—reforms that limited incumbency protection, imposed term limits, made Congress less partisan and more accountable, eliminated party control of the political process, and eased ballot access requirements. We asked that Bill Clinton speak out on behalf of these issues. Schwarz listened to us cordially and said he would take it back to the campaign. The Clinton camp never responded. Political reform was not of interest. What's more, if you weren't in the Democratic Party, you were on the fringe. If you were on the fringe, you and your issues weren't relevant.

Even so, Clinton's democracy shortcomings did not go unnoticed. Rev. Al Sharpton traveled to New Hampshire and joined Fulani at a press conference criticizing Clinton's failure to communicate on the reform issues. They pledged to hold him accountable when he came to New York for the primary there.

In March 1992 Clinton arrived in New York to campaign in Harlem, only to run into Fulani at Harlem Hospital; she stood on a chair and loudly silenced him. The encounter made news around the country, including a front page photograph of Fulani towering over a distraught Clinton in the Sunday edition of the *Los Angeles Times*. Clinton later described the incident in his autobiography, *My Life*, where he gave an anguished account of learning the ropes of brass-knuckled New York City politics. He wrote:

> In an ordinary Democratic primary, a campaign with this kind of
> support would be assured an easy victory. But this was not an or-
> dinary primary. First, there was the opposition. Jerry Brown was
> working like a demon, determined to rally the liberal voters in this

last, best chance to stop my campaign. Paul Tsongas, encouraged by his showing in Connecticut, let it be known that he wouldn't mind his supporters voting for him one more time. The presidential candidate of the New Alliance Party, an articulate, angry woman named Lenora Fulani, did what she could to help them, bringing her supporters to a health-care event I held in a Harlem hospital and shouting down my speech.[14]

While the scene at Harlem Hospital was surely an irritant, Clinton had bigger, more urgent fish to fry. He was locked in a competitive primary battle, the subtext of which was a contest between the progressive movement, represented by Brown, and the New Democrats, the Democratic Leadership Council's "centrist" camp, which was trying to meld globalism with a reconfigured New Deal coalition. Clinton, with all of his flaws (and paws!) was the DLC candidate. The reform agenda of a small and controversial independent enterprise appeared largely inconsequential at that moment. However, many of the reform issues we asked Clinton to support—to no avail—would surface again in a matter of months to drive the candidacy of Ross Perot, scuttling all the conventional wisdom of the 1992 presidential campaign.

In February, the political world was turned upside down. A Texas billionaire with a populist take on American decline announced his interest in running for president as an independent. "Let's go down to grassroots America where people are hurting," Ross Perot told CNN's Larry King. "Everybody's saying, why are we in this mess? First thing I'd like you to do is look in the mirror. We're the owners of this country. We don't act like the owners, we act like white rabbits that get programmed with messages coming out of Washington."[15] By late April, the polls had Perot, still formally undeclared, running ahead of the incumbent, President George H. W. Bush. Clinton was in third place.

The Perot candidacy put a new kind of pressure on Clinton and the Democrats. Having defeated Brown and eclipsed the Democratic left, Clinton hoped to project himself as the change candidate against the incumbent Bush. But Perot—even with the strange vacillations that took him in, then out, then back into the race—was a far more convincing change candidate since he took aim at both political parties. Clinton briefly had the upper hand when Perot withdrew in July, claiming that the Democrats had revitalized themselves. At that point, Bill Clinton called Perot on the phone and, he recalled, "congratulated him on his campaign, and said I agreed with him on the need for fundamental political reform."[16] His support for said reform never materialized.

Perot was out. But, putting the genie back into the bottle was not going to be easy. United We Stand America, Perot's support organization, called an emergency conference in Dallas to persuade him to get back in the race. Seizing the opportunity, the Fulani camp—with its base of African Americans and progressives—began to foster a direct relationship to this new base of independents, largely white and right of center. Fulani's campaign coordinator, Cathy Stewart, traveled to Dallas to offer up Fulani's candidacy as a place they could turn to if Perot did not reenter. Stewart was received cordially if inquisitively. The conference crowd was surprised, even interested, to hear about a black female independent running for president. But they were focused on one thing only: getting Perot to change his mind.

Once Perot got back in the race, Fulani used what platform she had to encourage Americans to vote independent, either for Perot or for her—either way to use the 1992 election to make a statement about the need to break out of the party system. Thus, the unorthodox left wing of the independent movement cast its lot with the Perot movement, as the DLC centrists beat out the orthodox left for control of the Democratic Party. The White House was about to change hands. And the center of gravity in independent politics was shifting.

The awkward contradictions were everywhere. The game was changing, but the traditional left had little connection to those changes. None put it better than Cockburn and Kopkind, who wrote in the *Nation:*

> The electoral system in America is now being convulsed by the broadest, fiercest voter insurgency in perhaps 140 years, and the left is watching from the sidelines. . . . The two formerly major parties are a shambles, institutions of government and the press despised, political authority disdained, and every measure of popular anger overflowing. And yet those who have long expected this

transformative moment to come, have organized and struggled for its arrival, are—if they are realistic—confronted primarily by their own irrelevance to this historic hour.[17]

In the end, Perot stayed in the race and captured 19 percent of the vote; Clinton won with 43 percent, and President Bush came in second with 37 percent.[18] Among independent voters as a whole, the results reflected the multi-ideological, multidimensional characteristics of this energized constituency. Independent voters comprised 27 percent of the electorate in the 1992 presidential balloting.[19] They split 30 percent for Perot, 38 percent for Clinton, and 32 percent for Bush.[20] Among independents who considered themselves liberals, 30 percent voted for Perot. For self-described moderate independents, 30 percent voted for Perot. And among conservative independents, 30 percent went for Perot.[21] Though one legacy of 1992 was to typecast the Perot movement as the "radical center" and the voters as "centrists," the roots of the movement were actually far more diverse. Independents of different ideological stripes gravitated to Perot, suggesting that his appeal went beyond traditional political categories to something more populist than parochial.

The newly empowered Clintonian Democratic Party had a tenuous hold on the country. The Democrats' return to the Oval Office came without an outright majority, and their congressional majority was reduced by ten seats. Not to mention the internal acrimony between the party's left and labor wing and its Clinton-led centrists, who would embrace more corporate-friendly and globalist policies.

The DLC still hoped to find common cause with the Perot movement, and in April 1993 it asked pollster Stan Greenberg to probe overlapping sets of interests between Democrats and independents. The DLC asserted that Clinton had to "take aggressive steps to reform and reinvent government." But the report found that Perot voters doubted Clinton's "ability to overcome the forces of inertia in Washington. From their point of view, the worst thing that can happen to President Clinton is that he permits himself to be captured by the Washington establishment. To underscore his 'outsider' credentials the president should push Congress harder to enact a program of radical change." The report concluded, "For President Clinton and the Democrats, the key to realignment is not mobilizing non-voters but converting unaligned voters." The DLC saw a new and durable majority in converting independents. "It is essential," they wrote, "that President Clinton offer Perot voters compelling reasons to join the progressive camp rather than congeal into a permanent third force."[22]

But the ardent globalism of the Clinton White House, complete with its support for trade agreements like NAFTA and GATT (which the Perot base vigorously opposed), combined with the Democrats' chronic distaste for political reform and tin ear for independent populism to put them at odds with the emerging independent movement and scuttled any chance of a Clinton-Perot coalition. Meanwhile, inside the independent political universe, with the Fulani forces drawing closer to the Perot base, the prospects for a new independent politic, drawing on a left/right, reform-oriented coalition, were looking up.

TWO

POPULISM VS. CENTRISM

THE COMPLICATED BIRTH
OF A THIRD PARTY

AFTER ROSS PEROT'S FIRST RUN FOR THE PRESIDENCY IN 1992, BOTH PARTIES TRIED to position themselves in a positive light with the 19 million Americans who had voted for him. It was, after all, the most significant independent presidential run in 80 years, since Teddy Roosevelt's 1912 Progressive Party campaign. This was brand new territory. Nearly one in five voters had rejected the major party options. A sitting president, George H. W. Bush, had been cast out. A new president was elected without a majority. Exit polling showed that if voters had believed he could win, Perot would have polled 40 percent of the vote.[1] The establishment feared that the Perot phenomenon could be merely the tip of an iceberg, and both parties looked for ways to grab a piece of the Perot magic.

The Republicans framed their 1994 Contract with America to draw Perot voters to their banner. This fueled their success in the GOP takeover of Congress in the midterm elections that year. Though Newt Gingrich's Contract fell short of the Perot mandate to "take our country back," it did call for a set of reforms to the congressional process (such as term limits for committee chairs) and for a balanced budget. Still, it steered clear of larger structural political reforms that were popular with Perot voters—like term limits for all legislators, campaign finance reform, and reining in the power of lobbyists on Capitol Hill. Meanwhile, the Clinton White House opened its doors to Perot. His adviser and son-in-law Clay Mulford pressed the Clinton team to initiate campaign finance reform, albeit unsuccessfully.[2]

United We Stand America (UWSA) was created to act as the permanent voice for the Perot movement. Among his followers, though, there was discomfort about settling in as an issues lobby. Some wanted to use the strength of the Perot vote to plunge into building a major third party, and they began to look for partners to take this plunge with them.

Notable among this group was Nicholas Sabatine III, chairman of Perot's campaign in Pennsylvania. In 1993 Sabatine reached out to Lenora Fulani, not long after she completed her second independent presidential campaign on the New Alliance Party (NAP) ticket. Unlike some figures in the post-Perot mélange, Sabatine viewed a new party in inclusive, coalitional, and from-the-bottom-up terms.

Sabatine, Fulani, and Fred Newman would be partners in shaping the new party. They were an unusual trio. Sabatine was a small-town lawyer from Wind Gap, Pennsylvania, with a thriving practice and a hunger for a political career. He and his prosperous neighbors had been drawn to Perot's clarion call for fiscal discipline, but he also had strong humanitarian and egalitarian values. Sabatine was, in many ways, the paradigm of a stable, middle-class, American independent. Fulani was born only 89 miles from Wind Gap, in Chester, Pennsylvania, but it was a world apart: predominantly African American, poor, and industrial. Fulani was the first in her family to go to college. She became a developmental psychologist to help black people ease the pain of everyday life. In 1978 she met Newman, whose postmodern Marxism and therapeutics radicalized her approach to psychology and human development. She also became a political independent. Newman was raised in a Jewish working-class family in the Bronx that was thrust into poverty by his father's unexpected death when Newman was a boy of nine. A Korean War veteran, he earned a PhD in analytic philosophy at Stanford University in 1962, studying under the renowned Donald Davidson. Throughout the 1960s he was fired from a series of teaching jobs after giving A's to all his students to help them stay in school and thereby avoid the Vietnam era draft. He and Fulani were quintessential, if entirely unorthodox, radicals.

Sabatine, Fulani, and Newman began a conversation. They led a series of informal group discussions on social policy. A cross-section of independents from the poor, black, gay, and progressive urban communities as well as small business owners and suburbanites took part. Social service spending, taxes, privatization of social security, welfare, and political reform were all topics of discussion. These traditionally polarizing subjects yielded new framings by bringing together "the overtaxed and the underserved" who shared a belief that the Great Society programs of the 1960s and 1970s had institutionalized poverty, not ended it. For everyone involved, political reform was paramount. One participant in these dialogues remarked some years later that if Congress conducted itself along these lines, the country would be a lot better off. It was against this backdrop that the Patriot Party's 1994 founding convention took place.

The convention was, among other things, a display of the cultural eccentricity of this new coalition. Rural Pennsylvania gun owners wearing Revolutionary-era tricorn hats chatted in the hallways with young urban blacks from the New Alliance Party sporting Malcolm X tee shirts. From the floor, some delegates called for the party's founding principles to support free enterprise, while others proposed affirmations of tolerance and respect for racial, ethnic, religious, and lifestyle diversity. Both resolutions were endorsed by the convention to convey the statement that left, center, and right were coming together. The defining moment, however, came when the convention considered how to describe the party it was in the process of founding.

Pollster and political scientist Gordon Black, who had advised Perot in 1992 and was among the initiators of the process that gave birth to the Patriot Party, proposed a set of principles describing it as a "centrist party." But the majority of delegates were not convinced. Newman vociferously objected to the term "centrist" because it introduced an ideological category into a party that was rejecting traditional ideology. The use of such categories, he argued, would lead to exclusion.[3] A heated floor fight broke out in which Sabatine's networks and the New Alliance delegates stood together against the centrist label. Caught off guard, Black warned the delegates to come to their senses. But, the delegates had their own sensibility. They voted to remove the term *centrist* from the party principles. Black and his delegation stormed out. Thus, the populists rather than the centrists became the axis of the new party.

There would be one more flashpoint at the founding convention: the election of officers of the party. Fulani had the majority of the delegates and was the obvious choice for vice chair, with Sabatine the obvious choice for chair. But, along with Newman, she had been the subject of a public controversy largely instigated by Democratic Party–allied competitors on the left.[4]

Sabatine appealed to Fulani and Newman to have her decline the vice chair position in the interest of party unity. Black's outraged departure would surely be controversial enough. When she was nominated from the floor for vice chair, Fulani declined the nomination, telling the delegates she would always do what was best for the party. The convention roared its approval. With that agreement in place, the populist Patriots were ready to cement the new coalition. The newly elected governing board was multiracial and politically diverse.

The *Nation* ran a series of articles by Micah Sifry covering the convention that seemed to mock the new partnership. The liberal left had never been comfortable with the New Alliance Party. Nor was it comfortable with the Perot base. In May 1992 Michael Tomasky had written in the counter-culture *Village Voice,* "Without saying that Ross Perot is Adolf Hitler, and without asserting that his supporters are the moral equivalents of good Germans, it is perfectly reasonable to point out that the types of people who are expressing support for Perot in America in 1992 reflect in many ways the types of people who supported Hitler in Germany in 1932. . . ."[5]

Nonetheless, the Patriot Party was off and running. The following year it held its second annual convention in Minneapolis, Minnesota—the site was chosen to promote the Minnesota Independence Party, which would later provide the platform for Jesse Ventura's independent gubernatorial win. The 1995 convention was broadcast nationally by C-SPAN and projected the unorthodox coalition at the heart of the Patriot Party. Chairman Sabatine, on the dais flanked by the national party's diverse executive committee, introduced himself and told the audience:

I am the chairman of the Patriot Party of America, the fastest growing independent party in the nation. This convention comes at an especially good time. Several weeks ago, a *Times Mirror* survey of American voters found that more Americans identify themselves as independents than as Republicans or Democrats. Thirty-seven percent of Americans identify themselves as independents while only 30 percent identify themselves as Republicans and 29 percent as Democrats. Simply put, independents are now the majority party in America. And I think our presence here today disproves another myth about independents, that we're all angry white men. Judging by our delegates I would say that independents, at least Patriot Party independents, are also angry white women, angry black women, angry black men. We are America here.[6]

Within 48 hours of the broadcast, three thousand viewers had called in. Some were Perot supporters signing on for a third-party effort. Others were African Americans responding to Fulani's statement that black America could increase its political power by becoming independent. This catalyzed a new phase of expansion at the party's grassroots.

While Sabatine was steering this wing of the Perot movement, state chapters of UWSA began an internal deliberative process on whether to continue as a lobbying organization or to take a next step and reorganize as an independent party.

Since the 1992 Perot campaign, Sabatine and others had kept up their contact with the UWSA network and lobbied strenuously inside it for the third-party move. As the summer of 1995 approached, plans for a UWSA national convention in Dallas were drawn up. A delegation of Patriot leaders decided to attend to push the party-building issue. The Dallas convention featured a panoply of Democrats and Republicans parading their wares before independents, happily overseen by Perot, to whom constant homage was paid. Rev. Jesse Jackson told the delegates: "The history of America is a history of citizens moving outside of parties and traditions, reaching for our better and truer self. . . . The great movements were always led by outsiders."[7] President Clinton's chief of staff, Mack McLarty, acknowledged that there were "disagreements between the president and Ross Perot"[8] but praised the movement "for seeking solutions rather than just pointing fingers at problems."[9] Republican House Speaker Newt Gingrich called the delegates "my fellow revolutionaries."[10] In closed-door workshops involving thousands of Perot supporters, the third-party question was debated. Sentiment was running roughly 70 percent in favor.

The Patriots hoped a more public display of support for party building would take things to the tipping point. Sabatine and Fulani convened a speak-out on becoming a third party. Three hundred UWSA members attended. Perot responded the next day by agreeing to meet with a delegation from the rally, which Sabatine attempted to negotiate but which never took place.

Nonetheless, Perot had begun to take the third-party idea seriously, considering a second run for the presidency geared toward party creation. In addition to the pressure from the Patriot Party and the ranks of the UWSA, he was being pushed in this direction by his former pollster Gordon Black and by billionaire businessman Tom Golisano, whose gubernatorial candidacy in New York a year earlier, backed by a repaired coalition of Black and Fulani, had won ballot-status in that state for the Independence Party.[11] Golisano and Black convinced Perot that a national party with ballot status in more than 25 states could be achieved via a presidential run in 1996.

In the meantime, Perot had become virtually incommunicado within UWSA and to the press. Then, early on the morning of September 25, CNN began promoting a previously unannounced appearance by Perot on *Larry King Live*. That night Perot made his move. "We're at a critical time in our country's history, and tonight we're going to start the process of starting a new party."[12] He said that he would undertake a national ballot-access drive to put a third party on the ballot. He would consider, but would not commit to, becoming the presidential candidate of that party. The drive would begin in California, where the deadline for filing was less than three weeks away.

California Patriot Party state chair Jim Mangia, a gay activist and New Alliance leader who sat atop a base of 8,000 registrants, strongly favored a coalition with Perot to establish the Reform Party in California. (During the first several days of the effort, it was called the Independence Party of California, but the secretary of state refused to allow that name because the American Independent Party already had a ballot line.)[13] Mangia, outspoken and charismatic, with a special flair for connecting with the Perot base, wanted to make the deal.

Sabatine was more circumspect. He supported the California play but wanted commitments from Perot and his chief of staff, Russell Verney, before agreeing. Other Patriot leaders (I among them) prevailed upon Sabatine to go ahead.

The day after the Perot announcement, Verney contacted Mangia and officially requested Patriot support for the Reform effort. Mangia hastily organized a press conference to announce the plan. But state law intervened. The California secretary of state informed Perot that the first several days of petitioning would be considered null and void due to a confusion over statutory deadlines. His only option to gain a ballot line was to register close to 100,000 California voters into the new party in 18 days—a much more difficult task than collecting signatures on a candidate-nominating petition. Perot was enraged but game, chalking the misinformation up to the "rough and tumble of politics. . . . The two parties don't want a new party."[14] Verney and Mangia were game, too. In short order, close to 7,000 Patriots reregistered into Reform while a heavily funded registration drive, backed up by a multimillion dollar media blitz paid for by Perot, succeeded in registering a total of 118,000 people in less than three weeks. Mangia and Verney filed the registrations in Sacramento. The creation of the Reform Party was underway.

Next, the effort fanned out into several more states whose deadlines were fast approaching. Patriot, which continued to exist as a separate entity with its own internal structures, provided assistance where Perot and UWSA were weakest—in the black and gay communities.

By the end of 1995, the Patriot Party and the Perot movement had formed an active partnership to create the Reform Party, even as some Patriot leaders—notably Sabatine, Minnesota's Phil Madsen, and Virginia's Ralph Copeland—were becoming very ambivalent about the coalition with Perot.

The Patriots called a national committee meeting in Virginia in February to discuss the relationship with Perot. The night before the national committee was to meet, Verney came to Virginia for a sit-down with a group of Patriot leaders.

The meeting crystallized the emerging divisions within the Patriot Party. Led by the Minnesota group, one segment of the party was becoming more vocal in their opposition to Perot and the Dallas team.

Later that night, Verney met privately with Fulani, Newman, and me. Our agenda was to discuss Perot's willingness to bring the Reform Party effort into the black and other minority communities. Verney, a veteran of Democratic Party politics, was far more familiar with black and progressive politics than most Perot movement activists. He had been the executive director of the New Hampshire Democratic Party in 1992 and was responsible for keeping Fulani out of the presidential debates in New Hampshire, a source of constant ribbing now that the two had joined forces. He had also been active in the bruising air controllers strike in 1981 in which the union—the

Professional Air Traffic Controllers Organization (PATCO)—was broken by President Ronald Reagan. Verney's experience with Perot had not dampened his traditional progressive outlook. He was amenable to Fulani's desire to bring black voters into the Reform Party. Asked about Perot's interest in an independent-black coalition two years later, Newman told the *New York Times*'s Frank Bruni: "I don't want to get caught up in portraying Perot as a screaming radical. That would be preposterous, and I would look like a fool. But I think he's open to the idea of inclusion."[15]

Increasingly strained by internal tensions, the Patriot Party turned its attention to the 1996 presidential race in earnest. It adopted a resolution empowering Sabatine to conduct further negotiations with the Perot team and directed its presidential search committee to intensify efforts to seek out possible Patriot candidates for the presidency.

Fulani attempted to interest Tim Penny, the former Minnesota congressman—a friend and a lone champion in Congress of a set of antipartisan structural reforms—to consider a presidential candidacy. Penny was not interested in running but pledged to Fulani that the Lamm Group, the recently formed circle of politicians considering the merits of independent politics (named for its convener, former Colorado governor Richard Lamm), would support the inclusion of the African American community in whatever moves it made.

Verney, representing Perot's interests as a possible candidate, was concerned that no move to propel Perot into the race be made prematurely and that any challengers from inside the Perot camp not declare an intention to run. When Fulani invited Verney to address the Patriot Party national convention in 1996 in New York, he readily accepted, seeing it as an opportunity to tamp down potential opposition to Perot.

Verney's planned appearance at the convention generated new media interest in Patriot, since the implication was that a Perot-Fulani coalition was in the works. This presumed left/right alliance was titillating to the press, which identified both Fulani and Perot (not to mention the 19 million Americans who voted independent in 1992) as "fringe." The *New Yorker*'s Michael Kelly wrote:

> Perot is now in a dance with a new set of fringe groups—this time on the leftward edge of politics. . . . And in the realm of the truly strange, the Reform Party has struck an alliance with Lenora Fulani, a Manhattan psychologist and two-time independent presidential candidate, and her beyond-the-fringe New Alliance Party.
>
> These dalliances and arrangements have almost nothing to do with ideology, and certainly do not represent any serious bonding between the left and Perot. Rather, they are based on the cold calculations of mutual need.[16]

Undeterred by the media's effort to hobble the left/right alliance, the Patriot convention voted to endorse the Reform process and to support the ultimate Reform nominee, whoever that might be.

By early summer the fissures inside Patriot were widening. The Minnesota wing of Patriot coalesced with a network of anti-Perot activists to promote the candidacy of a Democrat, Dick Lamm, leader of the aforementioned Lamm Group. Lamm was encouraged to run by Perot's Dallas operation, which hoped to strengthen the party's legitimacy by holding a national primary.

The primary was designed to be an experiment in direct democracy. All voters who had participated in the creation of Reform via signing a nominating petition or being a party registrant, or any voter who called 1-800-96-PARTY, would be eligible to vote in a computerized mail and phone balloting process supervised by the accounting firm Ernst & Young. Any announced candidate who polled over 10 percent in the first round would qualify to be on a final ballot. The winner in that second round of voting would win the Reform nomination. Lamm declared his candidacy.

Lamm's entry into the Reform primary set the stage for a power struggle. With his campaign managed by Tom D'Amore, top aide to former Connecticut Governor Lowell Weicker and an ally of Gordon Black, Lamm was, many believed, a Trojan horse for a centrist takeover of the Reform Party. Lamm and D'Amore believed that with the right stimulus, the party's rank and file would revolt against Perot and the Dallas group, and they could gain control of the party and its political philosophy.

Lamm made his appeal to two main camps in the party. First were the pro-centrist moderates. The other was the party's right wing, concentrated in California and other parts of the southwest.

While liberal on most social policy questions, Lamm held an alarmist, nearly apocalyptic, perspective on immigration, which was popular among Perot's most far-right base. His 1985 book, *The Immigration Time Bomb: The Fragmenting of America*,[17] argued that lax immigration enforcement combined with the trend toward multiculturalism was leading the United States to ruin.

But while Lamm courted these two elements, he was also aware that Fulani and her wing of the Patriot Party were a significant part of the Reform coalition.

In a phone call on July 28, Lamm asked Fulani for her support, presenting his record on civil rights. Fulani told Lamm that she welcomed him into the race, but that she was not prepared to endorse him or any candidate at that point. She encouraged Lamm to come to New York to meet. Lamm told Fulani that while she was an "important" person in the party, he was being counseled by D'Amore to stay away from her because of the "Farrakhan connection."[18]

Fulani told Lamm that she had been on black radio all week criticizing Farrakhan for his sympathies for Bill Clinton and the Democratic Party. Farrakhan was not the issue, she said; D'Amore's desire to keep black people out of the party was. Lamm insisted that he wanted an inclusive party and an in-person meeting with Fulani. The meeting never happened.

Meanwhile, a furor over the Perot-Lamm primary broke out in the press, most of it knocking Perot for controlling the nominating process. Headlines such as "Perot's Committee refuses to give rival the list of Reform Party supporters"[19] and "Sacrificial Lamm"[20] appeared. The *New York Times* editorial page recommended that Governor Lamm "call in former President Jimmy Carter to oversee this election."[21] The Lamm candidacy became a battering ram not just against Perot but against the populist wing of the party. Sabatine, abandoning his efforts to act as a buffer between the Perot forces and the Lamm forces, threw his support behind Lamm and publicly criticized Reform's process, intensifying the tensions inside of Patriot.

Once the ballots were counted and Perot was nominated with 65 percent of the vote (45,000 voters participated in the final round of voting), Lamm refused to endorse him, seeming to confirm suspicions that he was not committed to a long-term party-building perspective but had instead come in for a takeover play. Patriot remained intact, and its leaders became some of the most active spokespersons for the Reform party-building effort. While Perot was belittled in the press for showing "poorly" in the polls, the tactically important question was whether Perot would poll over 5 percent nationally, the threshold for establishing Reform as a recognized minor party, qualifying it for general election and convention funding in 2000.

Perot and vice presidential candidate Pat Choate ultimately polled 8.5 percent of the vote, well over the 5 percent threshold, though the Dallas contingent and Perot were disappointed with the results. After having been excluded from the 1996 televised presidential debates, they had resigned themselves to the goal of forming a party rather than winning the election. Still, they had hoped to break the 25 percent barrier, which would have qualified them as a major, rather than minor, party.

At a meeting of Reform Party activists in Nashville, Tennessee, in January 1997, an interim national committee was elected and interim officers were chosen. Verney was elected chair. Patriot's Jim Mangia was elected secretary. Sabatine, who had wanted a seat on the transitional national executive committee, was rejected as punishment for the divisive role he had played in the presidential campaign. Sabatine would soon leave the independent movement, reregister as a Republican, and go on to run an unsuccessful campaign in a Republican congressional primary in Pennsylvania in the spring of 1998.

Even after the Nashville meetings at which the Reform Party adopted the Patriot Party delegate selection process and its bylaws nearly verbatim—and Patriot's Tom McLaughlin became rules chair—Patriot remained intact for a time. There was some approbation about this from Verney, who worried that the Patriot group would turn into a dissident element within Reform. But Verney's concerns would come to naught.

At Reform's national founding convention in 1997 in Kansas City, Fulani hosted the first meeting of the 50 delegate members of the Black Reformers Network, with 300 white delegates attending as guests. In her remarks, she noted that the event marked the first time in the nation's history that black people were present at the founding of a major national political party. The audience cheered.

Two months earlier, I had circulated a resolution to the Patriot national committee calling for its dissolution. The resolution pledged its full support to the building of Reform and turned over the remaining funds in the Patriot treasury—$6,000—to the National Reform Party Organizing Committee. It passed unanimously. Patriot and its culture of left/right populism, inclusion, and bottom-up organizing was fully absorbed into Reform. It had played a crucial role in shaping the framework of the new party, in fending off the scheme to make it a platform for centrism, and in insisting that Americans of color would be welcome. Patriot's job was done.

THREE

AGAINST IDEOLOGY

THE RIGHT WING'S BRIEF ENCOUNTER WITH THE INDEPENDENT MOVEMENT

THE DAY AFTER THE IOWA REPUBLICAN STRAW POLL IN AUGUST 1999, I SPOKE BY telephone with Pat Choate. An economist of some repute, Choate was among the first to warn of the negative impact of globalization on American manufacturing. As the author of *Agents of Influence* and *America in Ruins,* and as Ross Perot's vice presidential running mate in 1996, he championed these issues, beating the drum about trade imbalances, the exporting of jobs, and the decline of American economic power. Distinguished and gentlemanly in an old-fashioned Southern style, Choate had stuck with the Reform Party after the 1996 campaign as Perot's Dallas team engineered its formal founding. He would later shed his gentlemanly exterior to steer a last-gasp effort by the Dallas inner circle to preserve its control of the Reform Party, but in the early days he was every inch the diplomat.

Choate told me that Pat Buchanan, his friend and fellow antiglobalist, conservative Republican, and frequent presidential hopeful (he had placed a strong second to George H. W. Bush in the New Hampshire GOP primary in 1992), had tanked in the straw poll (receiving 7 percent of the vote). Buchanan was thinking of leaving the Republican Party to become an independent. He was interested, Choate said, in seeking the nomination of the Reform Party.

I'd gotten to know Choate in the early phase of Reform's party-building efforts. In February 1999 I invited him to come to New York City to be a featured speaker at a national conference of independents, hosted by Lenora Fulani, Fred Newman, and me, entitled "The Meaning of Reform."

The evening prior to the conference, Choate had attended a performance at the Castillo Theatre of *Sally and Tom: The American Way*, a musical written by Newman about the slave Sally Hemings and her owner and lover Thomas Jefferson.[1] Choate, a Southerner who championed civil rights, told the conference that the message of the play—both a love story and a lament on America's failure to create a nation equal to its vision—was deeply connected to the topic at hand. "Each generation," he said, "has at least an opportunity, if not a challenge, of being reformers." Choate exclaimed that "the great idea of our time is political and electoral reform."

As soon as I got off the phone with Choate I told Newman about the call. Newman was wary. Buchanan was a right-winger, with febrile positions on immigration, affirmative action, and abortion. More important, as a veteran of the Nixon White House, he was a hard-core Republican with a reputation as a political brawler. Newman thought he had to be desperate if he was thinking of leaving the Republican Party for the scrappy netherworld of the Reform Party. Desperate men can be dangerous, we agreed.

Well aware of the concerns that we, as progressives, would have about Buchanan, Choate asked us to consider meeting with him if he decided to make the switch. Choate came to New York to make the case for a Buchanan candidacy. Political and economic reform could be the centerpiece of this partnership, Choate argued. In late September, Newman and Fulani agreed to meet Buchanan. The prospect of a high-profile, high-intensity coalition that shattered ideological norms and promoted political and economic reform was tantalizing, even if it was risky.

The face-to-face was shrouded in secrecy. Given Buchanan's fame and the growing speculation in political circles about his future plans, Pat and his sister and consigliere, Bay, were worried they would run into a reporter or political operative on the plane. They flew separately from Washington to New York.

Newman, Fulani, and I rode together to the Essex House Hotel across from Central Park in Manhattan and waited in the lobby, relaxing on a plush couch. It was late September 1999, and the leaves in the park had begun to turn colors. Newman was quiet. The setting had a kind of calm anonymity to it—one of the last moments of calm and certainly of anonymity that we'd have for many months. Later that afternoon, once the "secret" get-together was concluded, Buchanan went on CNN's *Crossfire* and leaked the fact of the meeting on national television. I learned a valuable lesson from Buchanan that day: It's always best to leak your own secrets; it gives you maximum control over the story.

Choate arrived at the Essex House shortly after we did, plainly wound up. The political tensions were evident enough, but Choate was sure this combination was just the kind of political dynamite the Reform Party needed to make its mark in the post-Perot era. As the architect of a potential political partnership between a set of controversial leftists with ample power in the Reform Party and a wayward right-wing populist with a major national profile gambling on a new political home, Choate styled himself as a kind of independent Henry Kissinger bringing Richard Nixon to China. (The irony that Buchanan had actually accompanied Nixon to China was not lost on anyone.)

When Buchanan blew into the main lobby of the hotel, with Bay and his wife, Shelley, in tow, he was a little sweaty, cracking jokes, acknowledging the surprised faces of hotel guests and staff, plainly out of his element. We all shook hands and said hello, then moved to a large table in the hotel's near-empty Garden Restaurant, where the sprightly floral wallpaper and pastel linens seemed ill-suited to the conversation. The next day reporters repeatedly asked me what we'd eaten. I could only remember that several of us ordered crab cakes.

The discussion began with Choate providing the Buchanans with a road map of our extensive networks within the Reform Party's National Committee and among convention delegates. Two months earlier in Dearborn, Michigan, the Dallas clique (with which Choate was, of course, aligned) had lost the chairmanship when Fulani threw her delegates' support to Jack Gargan, backed by newly elected Minnesota Governor Jesse Ventura. Fulani herself garnered 45 percent of the vote in the contest for vice chair. After Dearborn, Choate was convinced, however unlikely it might be, that Buchanan would need the support of the party's left wing to win the Reform nomination.

The discussion shifted to the party's nonideological orientation and how its focus on political reform of the electoral and governmental process together with the need for economic reform were the core values of the party. We instructed Buchanan that social issues (right or left) were not a part of the Reform Party platform and that any effort to introduce them would be a violation of what the party stood for. Buchanan said he had no problem with that.

But the political drama came toward the end when the dynamics inside Reform were discussed. By then, it was clear that the party's centrist faction, grouped around Ventura and the Minnesota

Reform Party,[2] would strongly oppose the Buchanan candidacy on ideological grounds, even though the party was supposed to be nonideological—a principle the centrists paid lip service to but in practice would not abide. Centrism *was* their ideology. Buchanan said he would work to appeal to Ventura and that element of the party nonetheless. But, he added with a chuckle, if we can't persuade them, "We'll roll 'em." Newman, no friend of the centrists and a target of their political defamations over the years, bristled at Buchanan's taunt. But he kept his cool, fixing his formidable gaze on our new partner. "You're coming in to seek the nomination of the Reform Party, Pat," he told Buchanan. "We'll support that effort. But, understand this. If you attempt to inject yourself into internal party politics, or if you attempt to turn this party into a right-wing party, we will destroy your campaign."

Choate paid the bill. And we all left. A few hours later, Buchanan was on CNN telling the story of the lunch.

Within 24 hours, a public debate exploded. On the surface, it was a routine airing of the left-right divide and the impossibility of overcoming it. But at another level, it raised questions about whether ideology itself was a valid component of the search for a new political voice.

Newman, a philosopher by training and a practitioner and developer of postmodernism, had observed the changing political landscape for years. In a little-noted book entitled *The End of Knowing*, published three years before the Essex House lunch, he wrote, "Left, Center and Right simply do not provide the

necessary categories of discernment (of any kind) in contemporary, complex, pluralistic, postmodern, world historical society."[3]
Nonetheless, American society was intent on preserving these
categories, even as the American people had begun to chafe at
their restraints. For the progressive wing of the Reform Party, the
coalition with Buchanan represented an opportunity to upend
traditional political alignments and to challenge the power of
ideology itself.

There were, of course, other calculations in the mix. The
Dallas crew, with Russell Verney at the helm, was looking for ways
to undermine newly elected chairman Jack Gargan and regain
control of the top spot in the Reform Party. They viewed Buchanan
as a potential ally in that effort, but a Fulani-Buchanan alliance,
complete with a "no-fly zone" over internal affairs, would torpedo
those plans. The endorsement also created a tactical opportunity
to develop a coalition between African Americans and blue-collar
white populists at the base around a new set of principles—political and economic reform.

Arguably, no independent movement in the United States of
America can grow without some rupture in traditional ideological alignments. Few were willing to press that button. But on the
night of the Essex House lunch, when Buchanan went on CNN and
mentioned that the meeting had taken place, the political reaction
was immediate. The tree of ideology was being shaken.

Newsweek's Matt Bai trumpeted the story in a piece headlined
"The Outlaws Come to Town."

By his own admission, it was an "anguishing" week for Pat Buchanan. As the commentator prepared to bolt the GOP's Big Tent to seek the presidential nomination of the Reform Party, even his spokesman quit in disgust. Meanwhile, Buchanan lunched at a Manhattan hotel with one of his new friends: Lenora Fulani, the longtime leftist and Reform leader. Once he had skewered her on his television show; now he listened carefully as she lectured him on ballot access. This was the new Pat Buchanan. Sure, you can still get him to rail against *Roe v. Wade* and the influence of "ethnic lobbies." But now Buchanan wants to put his social crusade on hold so he can build a coalition around issues—like fair trade—that appeal to all kinds of reformers. Fulani was impressed. Believe it or not, she says, "I will strongly consider supporting him."

Suddenly, despite a power struggle between Minnesota Gov. Jesse Ventura and party founder Ross Perot, Reform is the hottest ticket in disaffected politics. Why? For one thing, whoever wins the nomination will get about $12 million in federal matching funds; even in conventional times, that's a powerful draw. . . . Feeling closed out, and inspired by Ventura's coup, fringe candidates like Buchanan are staking out new ground on the campaign frontier: a vast plain where small bands of political outlaws live in separate camps, forging alliances via chat rooms and e-mail. It's not clear who's in charge, what the party stands for—or if there even *is* a party to speak of. But there's little doubt that Reform's candidate could have a dramatic impact on the election.[4]

Incredulousness quickly turned to outrage. Bill Kristol, editor of the neoconservative *Weekly Standard*, appeared on *Hardball with Chris Matthews*, apoplectic that Buchanan had lunch with these left-wingers.

> KRISTOL: Who is Pat Buchanan now . . . finding as his ally? Who did he have lunch with last Monday at the Essex House in New York?
>
> MATTHEWS: Tell me about these new friends.
>
> KRISTOL: Very fancy—fancy hotel in New York where all . . .
>
> MATTHEWS: Lenora Fulani?
>
> KRISTOL: Where the populists meet, you know, on Central Park South, the Essex House Hotel. He has lunch with Lenora Fulani and Fred Newman of the New Alliance Party.

Matthews acted stunned.

> MATTHEWS: He's making common cause with the far left?
>
> KRISTOL: Yeah, the disreputable far left . . .

Needless to say, this remark strains credulity since Kristol was not one to think there was a *reputable* far left! And, later in the show, Kristol boldly stated, "Pat Buchanan is having lunch with them. He is legitimizing them. And George Bush and John McCain and the other Republican candidates should say, 'Pat Buchanan has crossed the line. I don't want his support, let him go.'"[5]

A month later, when Buchanan formally announced his departure from the Republican Party and his plan to seek the Reform Party nomination, John McCain took Kristol's advice and said at a press conference, "Other members of my party, including the party chairman and others, begged him to stay. I strongly disagreed with that tactic, and as I've already said once, in the words of an old country and western song, thank God and Greyhound you're gone."[6]

Buchanan, seemingly impervious to the fulminations against him by fellow Republicans, made the cable TV rounds after his formal announcement on October 25, promoting the concept of the new coalition and the failures of the two-party system. He told Judy Woodruff on CNN that he thought the party structures were cracked and breaking down:

> And this is where an opportunity exists for a new party, a great new coalition of what used to be center, left and right, sort of populist, working class, conservative, traditionalist. And challenging, if you will, the incumbent establishment of both parties is one of the greatest opportunities I've ever seen. Maybe it won't come to be, but that's what we're trying to do, to build something new.

He went on to describe the relationship with Fulani:

> Now folks have quoted this black lady, Lenora Fulani, whom I used to have on *Crossfire* and "work over," in the vernacular. And she

was a left-wing individual and, I guess, a socialist. And she's been very supportive of me because "you stand up for the idea," she said, "that black folks have got to get away from the idea that they are victims and start relying on their own self-esteem. And by the way, Pat, will you support same-day voting, political reform, getting the big money out of politics?"[7]

If Kristol and the Republican right were astonished by Buchanan's move, the left was choking on it. This was now graphically on display, as it had been when Fulani first began working with the Perot movement in 1993. *Nation* editor Katrina vanden Heuvel discussed the Reform Party in October 1999 during an appearance (with me) on *CNN & Company:*

> You could say that the party stood for those things [being a non-ideological party that unites Americans around political and economic reform] when it was started. But today, it looks to many Americans like the party of loose morals that is becoming a vehicle, a kind of shell game that is being moved all around the political game board.[8]

Vanden Heuvel's "loose morals" accusation echoed a recently published piece by the *Nation*'s Bruce Shapiro titled "Buchanan-Fulani: New Team?" Shapiro wrote, "Already, Fulani has found media credibility as the ostensible left-winger in the Reform movement." He saw "pragmatic reasons for this strange new alliance. Buchanan would like Fulani's support; her Reform Party faction was strong enough to secure 45 percent of the delegate vote in the party's recent elections for vice chair. But it isn't just a case of mutual opportunism. The Buchanan-Fulani partnership exposes a dangerously corrupt corner of a third party founded on the promise of cleaning up US politics."[9] It was hard to tell whether the *Nation* was against corruption or against cleaning up politics!

From right to left, from the neocon Kristol to the *Nation* magazine crowd, there was a shared effort to disparage the alliance: No one should be permitted to cross ideological lines in this manner. And there was a subtext, too. Right and left seemed to agree that the most egregious aspect of the partnership was that Fulani and the progressive wing of the independent movement from which she hailed could be legitimized by a partnership with Buchanan, a strange premise given that the left hated Buchanan and the right believed he had betrayed them. Under those circumstances, how exactly would Fulani be legitimized?

After further negotiations among Choate, the Buchanan camp, and the Fulani camp, it was agreed that Fulani would endorse Buchanan's bid for the Reform nomination, that she and Choate would become co-chairs of the Buchanan nomination effort, and that Fulani would begin a process of introducing Buchanan to her party networks and to the African American community.

On November 11, 1999, Fulani flew from New York City to Washington, DC, for an endorsement press conference at the National Press Club. The night before, she called Rev. Al Sharpton to tell him of her plans and her intention to bring Pat Buchanan to walk the streets of Harlem and to meet Sharpton.

The National Press Club was a mob scene. The Buchanan brigades were out in force. Fulani traveled with a small team of aides. The press crowded the aisles and walkways. Bay Buchanan introduced Fulani as a "real trailblazer in third-party politics." Fulani, in a crisp and bright-red wool suit, took the podium and began by recalling what she learned in high school chemistry about the basic laws of magnetism: opposites attract. But, she continued, "what we're doing here today seems to put those laws to a very severe test. In traditional political terms, Pat Buchanan stands for all the things that black progressives such as myself revile. In traditional political terms, I'm certain that Pat would say the same thing about me. So how did we get to be standing here together, with me endorsing his candidacy? Because we have a common interest in overthrowing the traditional political terms."[10]

Fulani then went on to criticize the traditional black leadership, Democrats all, for insisting "that the partisan divide and the ideological divide as prescribed by the Democratic Party remain the Mason-Dixon line of American politics. But I refuse to stand behind that line, because I believe that until black America can be independent, it cannot and will not be free." The Buchanan brigades burst into applause.

She challenged the conservatism of the traditional left on similar grounds, reciting its fantasy of taking over the Democratic

Party. "But far from the left having taken over the Democratic Party, the progressive movement was taken over by the Democrats. The American left, like the black establishment . . . refused to take seriously the need to build an independent movement. They won't partner with politically incorrect allies, which is just what you need to do if you're to go up against the corruption of the two-party system."

She candidly admitted that Buchanan, "together with my good friend Pat Choate, made me an offer I could not refuse. And so I'm here today to accept it. I'm going to take Pat Buchanan to 125th Street in Harlem. We are going to have lunch at Sylvia's. I am going to take him to speak at Reverend Sharpton's National Action Network." So, Fulani concluded, "We are going to integrate that peasant army of his. We are going to bring black folks, Latino folks, gay folks, and liberal folks into that army."

Buchanan graciously accepted the endorsement, agreed to go to Harlem (though he never did), made a few jokes about their political differences during the Cold War, and turned the microphone over to Choate, who closed the program. The deal was done.

The *Wall Street Journal* editorial page weighed in on the endorsement of Buchanan the next day. With haughty but candid understatement given the hysteria surrounding the endorsement, the editorial stated, "In Ms. Fulani's opinion, 'we're going to integrate that peasant army of his' . . . Good luck."[11]

The endorsement and the ensuing public uproar over the ideological mismatch were probably the high-water mark of the adventure with Buchanan. It sparked a fierce public debate on the ideological divide. It challenged the "centrist" paradigm that has preoccupied elements of the independent movement since Perot's first run for the presidency, and which is still kicking around today in such enterprises as No Labels and Americans Elect. The Fulani-Buchanan alliance, short-lived as it was, was not designed to be a centrist partnership. It was to be a partnership of the left and right around a set of principles that defied ideological categorization. It was a provocation, a shot across the bow of ideology altogether. And it was a hard lesson in the institutional resistance to bringing Americans together across ideological lines and remains a matter of growing urgency as the wealth gap becomes more apparent and seemingly more unstoppable.

Ideology is a bedrock of modern politics and, surely, of the two-party system. The parties and the partisans cling to it and re-inforce it, in spite of its destructive power and even when it defies common sense or evolving realities. This is a huge and fundamental cause of the political disalignment that is producing so many independents.

Within a matter of months, Buchanan violated the terms of the deal with Fulani and Newman, collaborating with Choate and Verney to remove newly elected Reform Party chairman Jack Gargan and caving to pressure from Buchanan's donors to introduce a socially conservative agenda into Reform. Fulani withdrew her endorsement amid considerable media fanfare. Jim Mangia, who had grave reservations about the Buchanan alliance from the start, led a split national Reform convention in Long Beach, California, in the summer. The Federal Election Commission, in a stupendous act of political default, awarded Buchanan the Reform Party treasury of $12 million.[12] Still, Newman made good on his promise. Buchanan polled under a half million votes and had virtually no impact on the election. The independent uprising that had given Perot 19 million votes in 1992 and 8.5 million votes in 1996 deserted Buchanan. The independent movement was ill-defined, but it was not a force for social conservatism.

The independent presidential campaign that *did* have an impact in 2000 was Ralph Nader's on the Green Party ticket. Whether Nader's votes rightfully belonged to the Democrat Al Gore was a matter of fierce debate. But the results on Election Day 2000 sent the liberal intelligentsia into a tailspin when it decided that the Nader vote in Florida had thrown the national election to George W. Bush. Immediately, their mission became to put an end to independent politics in order to preserve the Democratic Party. Four years later, in 2004, when Nader ran again, the Democratic National Committee ran a concerted campaign to knock him off the presidential ballot in as many states as possible.

Just before Fulani publicly broke with Buchanan, Newman and I met with Nader's political adviser, Carl Mayer. This lunch, at the Waverly Inn, went unreported in the press. I don't remember what we ate, but we told Mayer about Buchanan's betrayal and invited Nader to jump in and challenge him for the still-undetermined Reform Party nomination. Win or lose, we counseled, Nader would come out the hero—battling the right, seeking to unify the independent movement, and building bridges between the left-liberals of the Green movement and the left-led populists of the Reform movement. Nader turned us down, with no explanation. It was surely a missed opportunity for him—one of many.

In November, his campaign fell short of the 5 percent mark needed to qualify the Green Party as a national party eligible for federal funds in the subsequent election. The total votes cast in 2000 for third-party candidates were well under 5 percent, less than a quarter of Perot's explosive 19 million votes just eight years earlier. Was it a public repudiation of political independence? Was the exploding independent movement that had mesmerized the country just eight years earlier burning out in a flash? The major parties certainly hoped so.

Most inside and outside the Beltway believed that the battles of the 1990s, which had left the third-party movement nearly defunct, had put an end to the growing unrest. In fact, that unrest was just beginning. On the day the Reform Party died, 35 percent of Americans were independents. Disaffection with government and disalignment from the parties would not subside. Instead, they continued to grow.

FOUR

FROM PARTY BUILDING TO ANTI-PARTY BUILDING

THE TWENTY-FIRST CENTURY BEGAN WITH A CONTESTED PRESIDENCY, A FIFTY-FIFTY political split among the American people, a third-party movement in a shambles, and a subdued electorate. In 1999 the Pew Research Center's typology survey reported that "the current national survey finds somewhat less political cynicism and fewer people highly critical of government than in the past, and especially in comparison to 1994. . . . A diminished appetite for political change is apparent, along with the moderating political attitudes we observed."[1]

Despite the tendency of hindsight to revise history, the election of the "compassionate conservative" George W. Bush, a

Republican, was not a significant shift away from the realist liberal Bill Clinton. After a decade of electoral rebellion, the voters were not looking for radical change.

The typology report summed up the political mood of the country going into the 2000 election thus: "the new politics of the American people looks more like the old politics. . . . Centrism, so characteristic of post-war American politics, is back. . . . Political cynicism, while extensive, has lost some of its edge, and clearly voters are less interested in outsiders and political newcomers than they were earlier in the decade."[2]

Likewise, the "outsiders," at least the more official ones, seemed remarkably less interested in the American people. Ross Perot had walked away from the antiestablishment movement he had catalyzed and returned to the business world. Jesse Ventura, halfway through his single term as governor, was devoting himself to Minnesota state politics, not leading an independent movement. Ralph Nader, battered by the liberals who had backed him and savaged by Democrats who believed he had cost them the White House, retreated largely to the role of consumer watchdog.

Three thousand independent voters from 42 states signed on to an Independent Appeal, circulated by the Committee for a Unified Independent Party (CUIP), calling on Perot, Nader, and Ventura to come together to lead a movement for independent political reform. None of the three responded. The abandonment was painful and disorienting. As the *Washington Times* noted: "No wonder a Committee for a Unified Independent Party exists. The Reform

Party is gone. The Greens are at the margins. Ross Perot is writing a book. Jesse Ventura is piloting a TV show. Ralph Nader is back to lobbying. And Pat Buchanan is back on *The McLaughlin Group*."[3]

Founded in 1994 by Lenora Fulani and myself to create campaigns and mechanisms for independent voters to gain some form of political recognition, CUIP began in 2001 to agitate and organize for the political reforms that had been the basis of the Reform Party movement. The goal was to foment an independent movement without creating another national political party. This would prove a long and arduous road. The handful of figures with the power to draw national media attention to independent politics were gone from the scene. Now grassroots independents had to rebuild a movement that barely existed, taking seriously the fact that 35 percent of Americans were independents because they didn't want to identify with any political party.

A sole bright spot in this otherwise dispiriting landscape, ironically enough, was the Independence Party of New York (IP), which soon became known as a kind of "anti-party" party. Founded in 1994 off the first wave of the Perot movement by a coalition between Perot pollster Gordon Black and the Fulani/Newman circle, the party ran Tom Golisano, upstate founder and CEO of Paychex, for governor on its ticket that year. Golisano received 217,490 votes on the line,[4] qualifying Independence to become a ballot-status party (50,000 votes are required in a governor's race).

Independence was an official political party. And New York was a "fusion state," meaning it permits political parties to "cross-endorse" candidates. A contender for public office can run as the candidate of more than one party; voters can choose which party line they want to use to cast their vote, and the votes are aggregated in a combined total. With this system (which is legal in only six states), minor parties can exert significant influence on the commitments of candidates and on the outcome of races, while providing voters with an opportunity to make a statement about themselves as well as about the candidate. Minor parties can also run their own candidates if they choose.

Over the preceding 50 years, minor parties had become a fixture in the New York political terrain. They tended to be ideological in their outlook and endorsements (for example, the Conservative Party, the Liberal Party, and the Right to Life Party), and they tended to be associated with, or even appendages of, one of the two major parties.

The Independence Party, born as it was in the crucible of a national uprising against corrupt partisan politics, envisioned itself as a different kind of party. Explicitly eschewing ideological positions on social issues, it styled itself as a vehicle for political and fiscal reform, leveraging the line and its endorsements to introduce reforms into the state's hard-core partisan practices, including its byzantine ballot access requirements, the ban on statewide initiative and referenda, supervision of polling sites by party appointees, and closed primaries, to name a few. The *New York Times* made note of the party's unique voice. "It does not exactly lean to the right or left. It does not take positions on issues like education, housing, crime or taxes. Indeed, its own literature acknowledges that many of its members sign up believing they are registering as unaffiliated with any party. Even that phenomenon sits just fine with Independence leaders, who have worked to create a tent so big, in their description, that it verges on the metaphysical."[5]

With the Fulani circle in on the founding, Independence would also reach out to communities of color to build the party's base. Fulani and Golisano campaigned together upstate in Rochester but proved an odd pairing. Golisano had none of Perot's pro-people populism. He was more of a technocrat, a small businessman whose business—payroll accounting services—had made him a billionaire. But, the energy of the moment and the enthusiastic response of New Yorkers to an independent option with a reform agenda pushed their differences into the background, at least for a time.

However, realizing this vision of the party would not come without a fight, Golisano allies soon wrote party rules that concentrated power in the hands of a chairman and executive committee, based on a weighted voting system tied to the gubernatorial results. With Golisano's popular vote heavily weighted in Rochester, the home base of Paychex, Golisano was able to control the chairmanship and all candidate endorsements.

Within the rank and file, though, there was resistance to Golisano's authoritarian control over the party. The Democracy Coalition, a group formed to overthrow his handpicked chairman, Jack Essenberg, proposed to rewrite the party rules to install local control over party nominations and other business. The ability of the coalition to succeed depended on their capacity to expand their networks on the elected state committee and to achieve sufficient numbers—even under the weighted vote system—to vote Essenberg out and rewrite the rules. In New York City, Cathy Stewart, a longtime Fulani and Newman ally, led the bottom-up infrastructure development, recruiting hundreds of Independence Party members (by 1998 the party's registration rolls had climbed to 134,000) to join the Democracy Coalition, run for state committee, and be part of the effort to reshape the party.

In Suffolk County, Frank MacKay, a local concert promoter-turned-Perot-activist-turned-Essenberg-antagonist, partnered with the Stewart clan, extending the coalition's reach through Long Island, Essenberg's main power base. After peeling away Laureen Oliver, a longstanding Golisano ally from Rochester, the Democracy Coalition's strength reached a tipping point. Essenberg's chairmanship was shut down in a series of parliamentary maneuvers by the state committee. Power swung back and forth in several court battles. In early 2000, MacKay was recognized by the State Supreme Court as party chairman; new rules were enacted establishing local control for each of the 62 counties; and a cross-ideological, cross-geographical executive committee was elected. It would guide the party's development as a force for political and structural reform. The Independence Party looked to be the embryo of what the national Reform Party had hoped to become: inclusive, reform-oriented, multiracial, bottom-up democratic, and, most important, independent. It would not permanently ally with nor bow to either major party.

AGAINST THIS BACKDROP, the New York Independence Party in 2000 found itself thrust into the midst of a high-stakes, partisan political battle. A Senate seat was vacant following the retirement of Daniel Patrick Moynihan. Both major parties had strong designs on the seat and strong candidates to carry their banner. Hillary Clinton, about to end her tenure as First Lady, would be the Democratic nominee. New York City Mayor Rudy Giuliani, a Republican, was seriously contemplating a Senate run. In this heavyweight bout, the Independence Party's endorsement and line could be decisive.

Individual leaders of the Democracy Coalition—whose politics spanned left to right—did not have uniform views on the Clinton-Giuliani contest. They had, however, reached a consensus in favor of holding a primary in which the membership of the party—now the third largest in the state at 172,000—would make the choice. This approach is wholly uncharacteristic of New York's minor parties, which create candidacies by fiat, based on backroom trades for patronage.

But, of course, there were political proclivities among the coalition's leaders. Though MacKay—officially neutral—had been "summoned" to the tarmac at East Hampton Airport in the fall of 1999 for a private moment with the President and First Lady, he inclined toward Giuliani. Certainly Giuliani hoped so, as the events of the week before the forum included an invitation to MacKay to meet privately with the mayor and his campaign manager, Bruce Teitlebaum, at Gracie Mansion. Oliver, who viscerally disliked liberals like the First Lady and favored law and order politics, was personally inclined toward Giuliani, too.

Jeff Graham, an Independence Party leader and the mayor of Watertown, New York, wanted to run for the U.S. Senate himself, which other Democracy Coalition leaders urged him to pursue. An articulate spokesman for the party's core agenda of political reform, Graham saw his candidacy—in a three-way primary matchup with Clinton and Giuliani—as an opportunity to leverage the political reform agenda and bring pressure to bear on the major candidates to warm up to the party's efforts to democratize the state's political process.

Finally, there were the Stewart-Fulani-Newman forces in New York City. As the left liberal wing of the coalition with a substantial base in the city's black and progressive communities, they were Hillary's most natural allies for the nomination and Giuliani's most natural opponents.

In 1997, when Essenberg attempted to maneuver the Independence Party line for Giuliani's mayoral reelection bid, Fulani had blocked the plan by announcing that she would run for the IP nomination for mayor and force Giuliani into a primary. Properly insecure about his ability to best Fulani in the city inside her own party, Giuliani had pulled back.[6]

Democratic Party elected officials around the state had noted the growth of the Independence Party and its eclipse of the Liberal

Party. The Independence line had already provided the margin of victory in several hotly contested local races. It had also added 109,027 votes to Charles Schumer's successful campaign to unseat Republican Senator Alphonse D'Amato in 1998.[7]

State Senator Marty Connor, the Democratic minority leader in the Albany legislature, was acutely aware of this realignment. In October 1999 he asked Democratic Party state chairwoman Judith Hope to meet with Cathy Stewart for a preliminary discussion about Hillary Clinton's proposed run for the U.S. Senate. The meeting was meant to be largely exploratory.

Connor hoped that he could shepherd a process that would increase Clinton's chances of getting the Independence line and set up a long-term partnership that would give the Democrats greater access to the state's growing bloc of independent voters—by then well over two million.

Stewart was more than agreeable. But she had a condition. A healthy future for the relationship of the Democratic and Independence parties—from her vantage point—rested upon the Democrats recasting their fractious relationship to Fulani. Stewart knew that the Democratic Party had made use of the left's anti-independent polemics against Fulani and Newman for partisan purposes. The party would have to acknowledge Fulani's integrity as an independent black leader. What better way to clean up the mess than to have the First Lady step in and end the demonization?

In early March 2000 the Democracy Coalition—on the heels of a state committee meeting at which Essenberg was formally removed as state chairman by a 97 percent majority and Frank MacKay was elected to take his place—began discussing its plans for the Senate race. The Erie County Independence Party would host a candidates forum in Buffalo to which all line-seekers would be invited.

From this point on, the exploratory discussions, feelers, and back-channeling accelerated. Giuliani and Clinton had to decide if they were going to seek the line, and if so, how they were going to relate to the different camps in the party. Given party leaders' consensus in favor of a primary, the candidates would also have to decide their primary strategy.

Giuliani's campaign manager, Bruce Teitlebaum, grabbed the bull by the horns. Yes, the mayor was interested in the line. Yes, he would welcome a September primary with Clinton. The Buffalo forum was penciled onto his calendar.

Teitlebaum had good reasons for his aggressive stance. The mayor's image was less partisan than the First Lady's, and thus he was more of a "natural fit" with the passionately antipartisan Independence base. Second, private polling numbers were showing Giuliani ahead of Clinton in an IP primary matchup. Third, he knew that the only way that Clinton could overcome her weakness with the IP base and be viable in a primary was to ally with the party's left wing—Fulani and Stewart. But, he knew that Fulani had been accused of anti-Semitism because of her support for the Palestinian cause. And that Hillary Clinton was weak among

Jewish voters, particularly since her photographed embrace of Suha Arafat, the PLO leader's wife, in 1999.[8]

Clinton's advisers were concerned that she was polling in the low 30s among Jewish New Yorkers, much too low for comfort. Teitlebaum judged that this weakness would make her wary of going to Fulani, whose support she would need to win an IP primary. No doubt, he planned to make an issue of it if a Clinton-Fulani alliance threatened Giuliani's ability to secure the IP line.

Teitlebaum decided that the issue to force was the primary. If the Clinton forces saw that Giuliani was unafraid to face her in a head-to-head matchup in September, it might force her out of the running altogether, since the primary would likely be her worst nightmare.

Some of Hillary Clinton's advisers thought the same thing. She was doing her own private polling. The numbers were showing Giuliani beating her among independent voters. Giuliani was gleefully stressing his willingness to have a primary. His commitment to appear in Buffalo solidified while the Clinton camp was mired in internal debate.

Bill Lynch, a black former deputy mayor of New York City under David Dinkins and an influential political consultant, called Fulani to ask for a meeting. Fulani filled him in on what was happening in IP, who was in control of the party, and what the Senate candidate selection process would look like. He queried her on her endorsement of Buchanan's presidential bid. Though tensions were high between Fulani and Buchanan by then, the actual break was yet to come. Fulani explained that Buchanan might be the Reform Party's, and since it was affiliated, the New York Independence Party's, presidential nominee. Lynch thought the Clinton camp was in too low a gear with respect to Independence. He and Congressman Charles Rangel, he said, thought the IP line could be very helpful to Clinton.

As the April 2000 forum drew nearer, State Senator Michael Bragman, a Clinton ally, asked Stewart how important she thought it was for Clinton to attend the Buffalo event. "It's mandatory," Stewart told him. What about the primary? he inquired. "Are you and your people in a position to prevent one?" Absent an explicit overture from the Clinton camp, Stewart affirmed, she could do nothing. Bragman countered that Stewart had no choice. "There's no way you'd go with Giuliani," he said. Stewart reminded him that Fulani had already endorsed Pat Buchanan. Enough said. Meanwhile, Bragman restated the Clinton camp's interest in avoiding a primary. Stewart restated her interest in Clinton repairing the damage done by left Democrats' attacks on Fulani. Bragman gave Stewart his assurance that there would be no Fulani-bashing at the forum if the First Lady attended.

On April 27, 2000, came Giuliani's bombshell announcement of prostate cancer. The media frenzy was relentless. Would he run? Would he cancel campaign appearances? Who would get in if he got out? There would be no final decision for several weeks. Yes, he would curtail his campaign schedule, and yes, he was still making the trip to Buffalo on April 29.

On the flight up to Buffalo, Teitlebaum later told Stewart, Giuliani's team was nervous. They pestered him. What if Fulani goes after you? The mayor was calm. I can handle it, he told his staff.

But Fulani had no intention of attacking Giuliani. Her question to the mayor, which received almost as much press attention as the coming altercation with Clinton, was about whether the mayor saw the Independence Party as a potential vehicle to reach out to the African American community. "I hadn't thought of it that way. The answer is yes," he told her in front of a stunned audience. "I haven't been able to communicate my message to the African American community as well as I should. Maybe it's my own inadequacies." He shook her hand after the question and answer session. The Independence Party audience was pleased with his performance.

As Giuliani was departing the airport in Buffalo, Clinton was arriving. The First Lady, clad in pink and pearls, took the stage. But behind her prim presentation, the gloves were about to come off. The Clinton camp had shifted gears. Fearful of a primary but equally fearful of Giuliani's strength if he were to receive the IP endorsement, Clinton had decided to bash the entire party in an effort to make it so radioactive that Giuliani couldn't accept its endorsement. From the podium, she exhorted the party to reject the "extremism of the right and the left." "Who does she think she is?" the audience seemed to mutter. Her proclamation that she wouldn't accept the line if Buchanan was at the top of the ticket was also badly received, even though, ironically, endorsing Buchanan had not been a popular idea within the New York party.

It wasn't until Clinton left the stage and entered the press room that her strategy became fully apparent: a full-scale attack on the party. Fulani was a left extremist trying to "hijack" the party, Clinton told the press. Yes, Fulani was the anti-Semite.

The room was in an uproar. By the next day's Sunday morning talk shows, the spin cycle was in full gear. George Stephanopoulos, Bill Clinton's former campaign press flak and White House special adviser now a political commentator, had been at the Buffalo forum whispering comments in Fulani's ear. On *This Week with Sam and Cokie*,[9] he pronounced Clinton's anti-Fulani play a "Sister Souljah." Fulani adviser Fred Newman later commented that it was far more likely that Clinton would be Fulani's Sister Souljah—a poster child for the coarse duplicity of liberal Democratic Party politics.[10]

Fulani responded to Clinton head on. "We don't appreciate a carpetbagger from Arkansas coming to New York and telling us who [is] and who isn't an acceptable black leader,"[11] she said. Fulani wasn't the only one who felt that way. Al Sharpton released a statement the next day:

> I've known Lenora Fulani for many years and she is a fighter for
> civil liberty, community empowerment and the dissolution of

economic injustice in our community. Lenora is a bridge builder, a coalition builder. And while we may not agree on everything, specifically her support of Patrick Buchanan and his conservative and traditionalist perspectives, it is erroneous and insensitive to associate her with negative politics. Though I share Mrs. Clinton's views on Buchanan—and find it strange that Mayor Giuliani, who attacks legitimate civil rights leaders, has no problem running on a slate with Buchanan—I do not share Mrs. Clinton's reported views that Fulani is an anti-Semite or a bigot in any form.[12]

In the days after the Buffalo forum, the press continued the melee. The *New York Post*'s Eric Fettmann, usually a harsh critic of liberal Democrats, praised Clinton's ploy and griped about Giuliani's friendly exchange with Fulani: "Rudy Giuliani admitting to his own inadequacies? Are we hearing right? But as welcome and refreshing a confession of fallibility as that was, why make it to—of all people—Lenora Fulani?"[13]

New York Daily News political analyst Joel Siegel headlined his article "Hil Looks Left for a Fight Now That Rudy's Ill."

Fulani called syndicated columnist and CNN *Crossfire* host Bob Novak—who had broken the story about her first meeting with Pat Buchanan—to tell him what had happened at the forum. Novak took his astonishment onto the air that night, when Democratic state chairwoman Judith Hope and McCain campaign adviser Michael Murphy were the show's guests. Novak prefaced his question to Hope by stating that in his nearly 50 years of covering politics, he had "never yet heard of somebody going into a party saying: I would like your nomination for the Senate, but I'm going to dictate the conditions under which I will take it only if you name somebody as the presidential front-runner. Can you give me a precedent for that in American history?"

Hope insisted that Clinton had taken "a principled position." Republican strategist Murphy then jumped in: "You know, this is grandstanding for cheap applause. That is all this is. Hillary Clinton has had a long time to attack Fulani or any other nutty extremist. She is not going to lay a glove on Sharpton. This is purely a totally insincere cynical maneuvering for some cheap applause, beating up a party nobody cares about with no support."[14]

Stewart reached Senator Connor the day after Fulani's press conference and Hope's appearance on CNN. "This is not a good situation," he told Stewart. Connor said he had not been in the loop for the final game plan. "They decided on a course," Stewart recalls Connor saying. "They knew they couldn't win a primary. They figured they could force Rudy out."[15] Connor was dismayed. His efforts at laying the groundwork for a Democratic/Independence partnership had been blown to bits by the Clinton cabal.

At a press conference, state IP leaders denounced Clinton's intervention. Laureen Oliver raked the First Lady over the coals. "If the First Lady was so concerned about the future character of this party, where was she when Jack Essenberg was trampling on the democratic rights of the members of this party? Where was the First Lady when Mr. Essenberg went to court to suppress a

75 percent majority of the state committee from enacting local control, exercising their party's rules and their statutory right to remove him? Where was the First Lady when Mr. Essenberg was aiding and abetting Donald Trump in Mr. Trump's efforts to 'hijack' the party?"[16]

Even Clinton's allies were circumspect about the play. Journalist Michael Tomasky, author of *Hillary's Turn*, a chronicle of the 2000 Senate campaign, wrote about the incident: "In truth, her saying this was not a big political risk. Given her troubles with Jewish voters, she couldn't afford to get within ten miles of Buchanan. And, given the fact that she and her husband had courted the party's leader, it was obvious that she'd summoned this courage only after it was evident to her that she wasn't going to get their line. Courage born of convenience is not courage at all."[17]

Several days after the blow-up, MacKay got a series of feeler calls on behalf of the Clinton campaign trying to determine if all the doors had been shut. They had. The Independence Party endorsed one of its own, Jeff Graham, for the U.S. Senate. Giuliani dropped out of the race. Buchanan won the Reform Party nomination, but after Fulani broke with Buchanan, the IP—at her request—disaffiliated with Reform and ran the Natural Law Party candidate John Hagelin for president instead.[18]

Hillary Clinton won the U.S. Senate race, but her relationship to the independent movement was damaged. For the Independence Party, it had been a test. The party had held its own in the face of partisan political maneuvering from both sides of the aisle and a political assault that reached all the way to the White House. Its left/center/right Democracy Coalition had held together. Its hard-fought independence had been preserved, for the moment. In the years to come, however, the pressure to do otherwise would become increasingly intense.

FIVE

BLOOMBERG'S DILEMMA, PART I

IF THERE IS ONE PERSON WHOSE NAME IS MOST ASSOCIATED WITH INDEPENDENT politics in the 1990s, it is Ross Perot. In the subsequent decade, it became Michael Bloomberg, the three-term mayor of New York City, the speculative but never actual independent presidential candidate, and the sometimes promoter of nonpartisan political reform.

I came to know Michael Bloomberg during that decade. It is widely acknowledged that were it not for the Independence Party of New York City, he would not have been elected mayor in 2001, gaining the political platform through which he became an influential national figure. The ten-year partnership between the Independence Party and Bloomberg spawned many things, including several fierce battles to reform the partisan New York City municipal election system, a split in the Independence Party between its city branch and the state leadership, Bloomberg's emergence as a nationally known independent, and constant conflict between the Democratic Party and the Independence Party that shaped Bloomberg's tenure in City Hall.

This Bloomberg story is not about his wealth, though having a personal fortune of some billions of dollars is not inconsequential. This Bloomberg story is not about his mayoralty, which has been widely documented in the press. This Bloomberg story is not about his personal life, or his philanthropy, or his business acumen, all of which I know next to nothing about except what I read in the papers. Rather, it's about a powerful and ambitious man who waded into the waters of a small but consequential independent political universe, got himself elected mayor of the most important and most partisan city in the world as a result, and spent a decade reaping the benefits and managing the dilemmas produced by that alliance.

Most people—including independents—don't know *that* Bloomberg story. But I'd argue it's the most fascinating one—this dynamic, bottom-up movement that put an independent in City Hall and a new face on "independence" in America.

CATHY STEWART, THE CITYWIDE COORDINATOR of the Independence Party (IP), and I made a visit to Bloomberg LP, on 59th Street and Park Avenue in Manhattan, in early March 2001. After a tour of the headquarters with Bloomberg's political attaché, Kevin Sheekey, the three of us arrived at the door to a small office, complete with a Bloomberg machine and Bloomberg himself.

Bloomberg was very affable as I recall, even slightly self-effacing. We discussed—ironically enough—a *New York Times* article published that day about the City Council's attempt to overturn term limits, in which Cathy Stewart was quoted protesting the whole idea. "Term limits foster competition and bring new blood into government," she had told the *Times*. "They break up institutionalized incumbency protection eliminating the career politician and the patronage system that nourishes him or her."[1] Sheekey and Bloomberg shared that view at the time.[2] The conversation moved quickly to the Independence Party, its roots in a cross-section of communities, and its emphasis on nonpartisan political reform. This was all new terrain for Bloomberg. At one point he asked us about his mayoral candidacy. "Do you think I should run?" he said. "It depends on *how* you run," I replied, explaining that if he ran as an independent reformer—and sought the Independence Party's backing on that basis—it would be a race worth running.

Bloomberg and Sheekey had no doubt heard through the political grapevine that the IP leadership were wild-eyed radicals. My guess is that Stewart and I allayed some of their worst fears. We both wore expensive suits to the meeting. We knew the independent landscape like the back of our hands. And our team had a controlling interest in a very desirable piece of New York political real estate.

There was also no doubt that Bloomberg and Sheekey were interested in the Independence Party. Nearly 20 percent of city voters were registered as independents.[3] Bloomberg was planning to run as the candidate of the Republican Party.[4] But Democrats—with a five-to-one registration advantage over Republicans[5]—would be loath to vote for Bloomberg as a Republican. New York is a fusion state in which election law permits candidates to run on more than one party line and to aggregate those votes. Having his name on the ballot twice, with voters having the option of pulling the Independence lever, would be a huge advantage. Besides, unlike many political operatives whose entire worldview is shaped by partisan allegiance, Sheekey was unique. Bloomberg's money alleviated the need to be tied to a political party. Plus, Sheekey had a genuine sense that the country's political tides were turning away from traditional partisan politics. A Bloomberg candidacy affixed to the Independence Party, broadcasting its concept of nonpartisan political reform to upend machine control of policymaking, could frame an appealing brand. Sheekey could craft that framework with political consultant David Garth (who had strategized John Anderson's independent presidential campaign in 1980) for a Bloomberg bid.

Though Bloomberg also tried to win the backing of the Liberal Party, which gave Rudy Giuliani his winning margin over Mayor David Dinkins in 1993,[6] it rejected the Bloomberg option. The Conservative Party was off limits because Bloomberg was not a conservative. The union-based Working Families Party (WFP) was tethered to the Democrats and thus a nonstarter, at least in 2001. The Independence Party endorsement would be key.

The next day Bloomberg sent a messenger with two inscribed copies of his book *Bloomberg on Bloomberg* to Stewart and me, thanking us for our contribution to improving civic life.

For the Independence Party, the prospect of a partnership with Bloomberg was complex. The Rudy Giuliani years had been devastating for race relations in New York City. City leaders of IP had blocked Giuliani from running on the Independence line in 1997. The IP's base in black, Latino, and poor communities had grown substantially. And with the Giuliani era coming to a close (term limits banned him from a third run), the Democratic Party—which reigned supreme in those communities—had every hope and expectation that its nominee would be sitting in City Hall in the new year. They were already writing the script to reverse (even revenge) the racialism of Rudy's tenure. The more natural partnership would have been between the IP and the Democrats.

In a sane world, with the Democratic leadership pulling out every stop to ensure a victory, that would have meant securing Independence Party support for its candidate. This endorsement would give the Democrats access to the growing pool of independent voters, which by 2001 numbered 52,000 IP members and 699,000 nonaligned independent New Yorkers. But in the bestial world of Big Apple politics, sanity rarely prevails. Indeed, consultants for Mark Green, expected to be the Democratic nominee, recommended that he seek Independence Party support for his mayoral bid. (Green was elected public advocate with IP backing in 1997.) But, in a common story line, a major union leader nixed the idea. IP's top New York City leadership—notably Fred Newman and Lenora Fulani—were progressives who had defied the leftist orthodoxy on numerous fronts, especially by opting for an independent, rather than a Democratic, electoral strategy. They had organized among the poor, not within the unions. They had created an array of social service institutions supported by the business community, not by government funding. This made them persona non grata among many left Democrats and unions.

For all his social liberalism, a partnership with Bloomberg would be controversial, especially in the context of a change election in which, after an eight-year drought, the liberal left stood to send a Democrat to City Hall. The benchmark for the IP was whether such a partnership could advance the party's agenda for nonpartisan reform and, thereby, its influence on the New York political scene. Since the founding of the Independence Party in 1994, the New York City wing had led the party's reform activism, first in a protracted internal battle when the Golisano clique was overthrown and local control was installed inside the party, and then in its embrace of independent redistricting, the right to initiative and referenda and nonpartisan elections.

In the early spring, as discussions with the Bloomberg team continued, IP's general counsel, Harry Kresky, a renowned election law attorney, presented a plan to Newman and me for a shift from the longstanding, partisan design structure of New York municipal elections to a nonpartisan one. Under the city's charter, the mayor could impanel a Charter Revision Commission to put the question to the voters. This reform would eliminate party control of the nominating process and open first-round balloting to the city's 750,000 independents.

Control of nominations is the bread and butter of party life, even in minor parties. As political commentator Walter Karp observed in *Indispensable Enemies:* "By their control over nominations, organizations and their leaders hold the careers of elected officials in their hands, for they can deny them renomination, remove them from public life or bar their further political advance."[7] It would take a very independent-minded mayor to pursue this with any chance of success. Newman and I discussed this with two political consultants, William O'Reilly and Susan del Percio. O'Reilly and del Percio, both Republicans, encouraged us to take up the issue with Bloomberg. Kresky, Stewart, and I pursued nonpartisans—along with a full program of reforms—with Sheekey and Bill Cunningham, the campaign's new political adviser. Both Sheekey and Cunningham were veterans of the respected New York political team assembled by U.S. Senator Daniel Patrick Moynihan—in other words, they were go-against-the-grain Democrats.

At our next meeting with Bloomberg, Newman, Stewart, and I presented him with a proposal for nonpartisan elections. Cunningham was there and obviously cool to the idea, though he deferred to his new boss. An old hand at Democratic politics, Cunningham knew that any support for this reform would kick up a hornet's nest of opposition from the Democratic machine. But nonpartisan elections were right up Bloomberg's alley. He had already gotten a taste of clubhouse politics in his short stint as an unannounced candidate, and he knew it was petty, turf-ridden, and unspeakably mediocre. He had no loyalty to any political machine, for which his opponents—with their tin ears to the growing public repugnance toward partisanship—were quick to criticize him. For them, partisanship was a virtue. But Bloomberg immediately grasped that an open system allowing nearly one million New Yorkers to vote in a public primary would be a huge step away from clubhouse control.

There was only one thing Bloomberg didn't understand. Why would the Independence Party, which would forfeit its ballot line under a nonpartisan system, be advocating for such a reform? Newman explained it to him. "We're an anti-party party," he told Bloomberg. "We came into existence to fight the party system. We *want* to be put out of business." At that meeting, we agreed that the Independence Party would move toward an endorsement of Bloomberg, and, if elected, he would work to introduce nonpartisan elections to the most partisan, brass-knuckled, party-controlled city in America.

On June 5, Bloomberg announced his candidacy in a series of TV commercials designed by Garth. His first press conference as a mayoral candidate was two days later on the steps of City Hall where he, I, and 50 Independence Party members jointly pledged our support for nonpartisan elections. "What the electoral process should be about is letting everybody have an equal say. . . . You've got to get rid of the partisan politics and party bosses who really limit the public's choice," Bloomberg proclaimed.[8]

Two weeks after he launched his campaign, IP leader Lenora Fulani, an outspoken critic of the Democrats' hold on the black community, threw down the gauntlet to their presumed monopoly over the black vote and endorsed Bloomberg. The *Black Star News* reported Fulani's statement: "Mike Bloomberg is the kind of candidate the black community likes to vote for. He has liberal values and a genuine concern about education, public health, and social justice. But more than that, he's an independent. That's why the IP endorsed him. And that's why I think he's far and away the best mayoral candidate for black New Yorkers."[9] She told Cedric Muhammad of BlackElectorate.com, "If we give him 20 percent of the vote, then we win because it makes the black vote an unpredictable vote in the future. The black community doesn't realize how valuable unpredictable votes are."[10] And with teams of volunteers, she campaigned vigorously in black churches and on the streets and subway platforms in African American and Caribbean neighborhoods, explaining how voting independently gave the black community more power.

The Fulani endorsement of Bloomberg as an independent did not sit well with the Democrat-aligned *Amsterdam News*, the black paper of record in New York City. It published a harsh editorial in late July accusing Bloomberg of trying to buy the election. "I've got money . . . elect me and I will give you some," was how that paper boiled down his campaign message.[11] The Democratic Party was confident that black voters, tired of eight years of Giuliani rule, could be counted on to support the Democratic Party nominee, whoever that turned out to be.

There was a tense four-way primary taking place for the Democratic nomination, among Public Advocate Mark Green, Bronx Borough President Fernando Ferrer, Comptroller Alan Hevesi, and Council Speaker Peter Vallone. Their attacks on Bloomberg for allying with the Independence Party had already begun. The *New York Daily News* reported: "And three of the four Democratic mayoral hopefuls this year [Hevesi, Green, Ferrer] have ruled out seeking the Independence Party's line on the November ballot because of Fulani or the party's ideology."[12] The Democrats were trying to weaken Bloomberg with a double-barreled assault; brand him simultaneously as an out-of-touch Republican billionaire while linking him to a black female radical who, though popular in the African American community in no small part because of her years creating privately funded youth development and antiviolence programs in the poor communities, was illegitimate in the eyes of the Democratic establishment.

Bloomberg, in full campaign mode, was introducing himself to New Yorkers, sampling pizza slices in Bay Ridge and dim sum in Chinatown. He penned an editorial in *New York Newsday* entitled "Get Party Politics out of City Hall," which reiterated his support for nonpartisan elections. Commenting that war should not be the sole province of generals, Bloomberg added, "I would say that democracy is too important to be left to the politicians. Let the people in."[13] State Democratic Party chairwoman Judith Hope had a brusque reply. "Without the network of support that political parties provide, only billionaires like Michael Bloomberg will be able to mount campaigns for election here in New York City."[14]

Primary day was scheduled for September 11. But the relative calm of the 6 A.M. poll openings was shattered at 8:46 A.M., when the first of two planes flew into the Twin Towers of the World Trade Center, killing nearly 3,000 people. As the city and the country struggled to regain its footing, all campaigning was suspended. But not for long. Even a tragedy as great as 9/11 could not halt the march of the political machine. As Bloomberg pollster and political consultant Douglas Schoen later commented, "Not even the trauma of 9/11 and the unifying reflex it triggered could overcome the powerful partisan pressures that were pulling the country apart."[15]

Primary day was rescheduled for September 25, and campaigning resumed in a subdued atmosphere. Ferrer and Green were the top vote-getters in the Democratic primary, but neither one received 40 percent of the vote, forcing a run-off election for October. During the run-off campaign, a flyer surfaced with a grotesque cartoon showing Ferrer kissing Al Sharpton's rear, to frighten white Democratic voters into supporting Green by raising the spectre of a black radical calling the shots from inside City Hall. (This is, unfortunately, a popular attack strategy in Big Apple politics.) Green won the run-off, but the collateral damage could not be contained.

Black leaders and the black community were up in arms. The Green campaign vigorously denied responsibility for the flyer, and the divisions inside the Democratic Party became acute. Unity rallies were called. The *New York Times* reported on October 20, 2001: "In a measure of the importance the party has attached to winning City Hall back after Mayor Rudolph W. Giuliani's term, the hastily called event was also attended by both New York senators, Charles E. Schumer and Hillary Rodham Clinton, as well as the national Democratic chairman, Terry McAuliffe, and the state Democratic chairman, Judy Hope."[16]

The *Amsterdam News*, deciding it was payback time, switched horses and endorsed Bloomberg. All the groundwork Fulani and her team had laid—pounding the pavements of Harlem and black Brooklyn and persuading influential black media personalities to support the independent campaign for Bloomberg—now came into play.

After trailing in the polls for the entire five-month campaign, Michael Bloomberg defeated Mark Green by just 35,000 votes,[17] the narrowest margin in a New York City mayoral race in 96 years. Bloomberg carried 25 percent of the black vote.[18] Bloomberg polled 59,091 votes on the Independence Party line,[19] almost double his margin of victory. Sheekey later said he collected the returns on a yellow pad, calculated the margin, and circled the IP numbers. Without the Independence Party, Bloomberg would not have become mayor.

New York City had a new chief executive who was neither a Democrat nor a politician. That was surprise enough. But it also had a new "major" minor party, the Independence Party. Joel Siegel of the *New York Daily News* three days after the election opined, "Meet one of the city's new kingmakers: Lenora Fulani."[20] A public forum six weeks after the election at the National Black Theatre in Harlem was entitled "What Did Black New Yorkers Gain from the 2001 Mayoral Election?" Three hundred people attended, not a single elected official among them. Fulani and a group of popular black radio personalities—Mark Riley, James Mtume, Bob Slade, Bob Pickett—led a spirited two-hour discussion about the significance of the Bloomberg victory. Said Slade, "We have broken the chains of political dependency on the Democratic Party. . . . You saw it happen. We can take it further." The Independence Party had not only elected a new mayor. It had engineered a minor but consequential revolt by African Americans against the Democratic Party.

For his part, Bloomberg was suddenly thrust into the position of governing a city that, for all practical purposes, is run by the Democratic machine. His advisers counseled that he needed to make peace with that machine at the earliest possible moment. The morning after the election he had breakfast with Ferrer. Later that day, at the One Hundred Black Men 22nd Annual Gala Benefit in midtown, Bloomberg met briefly with Al Sharpton. Conspicuously, he did not call on Lenora Fulani. It seemed obvious that the Democratic Party had delivered a message to Bloomberg: *You may have been elected without us. But you cannot govern without us. And there will be no more talk of political independence in the black and Latino communities. Understood?*

The Independence Party, meanwhile, searched for some definition of its own standing with the mayor it had just sent to City Hall. Though hundreds of IP activists had worked the streets and phone banks to pull the vote for Bloomberg and the IP vote had made him mayor, tensions had escalated between the Bloomberg team and the IP in the weeks leading up to the election, exemplified by one incident in late September.

After the shock of 9/11, Fulani received inquiries from supporters and colleagues asking for her thoughts on the attack on the World Trade Center. In response, she had sent a personal email strongly condemning al-Qaeda's criminal attacks. In the note, she suggested that America had been "made vulnerable" by a history of the U.S. government's "aggression and arrogance." The *New York Post*, owned by right-wing tabloid king Rupert Murdoch, got a hold of the email and grabbed the opportunity to make trouble. The *Post* sent the Bloomberg campaign a copy of the email and asked for comment. Bill Cunningham called Cathy Stewart and directed her to have the IP repudiate Fulani's note. Stewart refused.

The next day the *New York Post* ran a story headlined "Mike Raps 'Backer' Fulani Message," which included a statement by Bloomberg. "If the leadership of the Independence Party does not renounce Ms. Fulani and her anti-American views, then I will not campaign on their line and I will urge people not to vote for any candidate on that line, myself included."[21] Cathy Stewart sent a letter to the mayor on September 26. "It should be clear by now that we do not intend to disavow Dr. Fulani. That is not how we operate.

What's more, we do not permit others to dictate to the party how we conduct our affairs," Stewart wrote.[22]

Cunningham had overreached and the response from the IP was swift. Bloomberg had every right to disagree with Fulani's remarks if he chose. But he did not have the right to inflict damage on the party that had nominated him by deliberately trying to drive down its vote total. Far from accepting the announcement that Bloomberg would campaign against his own candidacy on the IP line, the IP sought legal redress. IP attorneys served papers on the Bloomberg campaign, asking the court to remove Bloomberg from the party's line and allow it to choose another candidate since he was, in essence, leaving IP without a candidate. This was not the response the Bloomberg team had anticipated.

The matter never made it to the courtroom. Senate Majority Leader Joe Bruno, a Republican with ties to Independence Party state chairman Frank MacKay, negotiated a settlement. The Bloomberg team agreed to continue to campaign for votes on the IP line, a "make-up" press conference was designed, and the suit was withdrawn.

The episode, though, combined with the constant pummeling by the *Post* and by Democratic leaders, put a strain on the IP's relationship to the mayor. As Cunningham assumed the role of communications director for the new administration, and Democrat establishmentarians from former Mayor Ed Koch's administration were brought in to handle the transition, independents wondered how welcome they would truly be at City Hall.

In search of answers, Newman, Stewart, and I met with Cunningham in January 2002 in the basement chapel at City Hall. Cunningham's tone was respectful but reserved. Newman was characteristically direct. He told Cunningham we were not interested in any patronage jobs or administration positions, only the reform principles that had brought us together in the first place. But there was an elephant in the room. Newman asked Cunningham whether the IP in general, and Fulani in particular, were going to be considered persona non grata by City Hall. Cunningham paused, a rarity for the quick-witted and sharp-tongued political operative. No, he said, that won't be the case. With that, Mike Bloomberg, registered Republican, cozying up to the Democrats but elected by the independents, began his tenure as the 108th mayor of the City of New York.

IN JUNE 2002, SIX MONTHS AFTER taking office and completing his takeover of the public school system,[23] Mike Bloomberg announced the formation of a Charter Revision Commission (CRC) to explore changes to the city's charter, including consideration of a nonpartisan election system. Bloomberg explained the commission's mandate: "When you have a small group of people voting in the primaries, a small group of people at best define what the public's choice is—and that's just not as democratic as it should be."[24] Under New York City law, mayors can empower charter commissions to consider amending any and all aspects of the city's governing charter. By law, such commissions must hold public hearings and then place their recommended changes on the ballot for the public to approve.

Led by state party chairman Herman "Denny" Farrell, the Democrats retaliated against the mayor's push for nonpartisan reform with scorn. Serena Torrey, a spokeswoman for the New York State Democratic Party, staunchly defended the party system. "Party politics and partisan elections have played an enormous role in bringing thousands of New Yorkers into the political process," she said.[25] The public advocate and city controller, both Democrats, piled on.

Nonpartisan elections, a relatively innocuous reform, are the standard in 75 percent of major U.S. cities. With nonpartisans, electoral coalitions are both less durable and more fluid, forming and reforming around particular candidacies in the interests of the coalition partners but not necessarily or inevitably in the interests of the party. This, apparently, was the rub of enacting them in New York.

As political critic Walter Karp once explained, party organizations are engaged in a "constant endeavor to prevent the organization from fragmenting into an unbossed coalition of independent local coalitions. . . . If it fragmented this way, the would-be party bosses would lose control of the party and with it control over nominations and political power itself."[26] And so the party establishment unleashed its full fury on the unsuspecting Bloomberg.

The mayor soon released the names of his thirteen commission appointees, including Independence Party chief counsel

Harry Kresky. Quickly, Rupert Murdoch's *New York Post* accused Bloomberg of paying "an ugly debt"[27] to the Independence Party, calling on Bloomberg to rescind the appointment. Bill Cunningham, speaking out in defense of Kresky, called the criticism "ridiculous."[28] Meanwhile, top commission aides Bradley Tusk and Anthony Crowley, feeling the heat, paid Kresky a visit at his law office. They asked him to resign from the commission, which was all of three days old, suggesting that his participation would distract from the issue at hand. Polite and noncommittal, Kresky thanked them for their concerns. Then he wrote a letter to the mayor, affirming his loyalty to Bloomberg and to the nonpartisan cause but refusing to step down. "This effort has, already, generated substantial opposition from powerful special interests. My resignation would give a signal that the commission is not willing to stand up to them," he wrote.[29] There was no more talk of resignation.

In early August the People's Coalition for Nonpartisan Municipal Elections, instigated by Fulani, held a press conference on the steps of City Hall. It consisted of 75 community activists, mainly black and Latino, who supported the reform. Lonnie Shockley of Fathers United for Solutions Through Education told reporters, "Unfortunately for many of us, our two-party system is not the voice of the majority or many people." Anthony Miranda, the executive director of the National Latino Officers Association, added, "This is going to be a door opener that tells people that I don't have to wait for the Republican, the Independent, or the Democratic primary." Dr. Jessie Fields, a Harlem physician and vice chair of the Manhattan Independence Party, said, "Nonpartisan mayoral elections would be greatly beneficial to the Harlem community because it breaks up control, machine control, partisan machine control."[30]

The first public hearing on the proposed reform was held in Brooklyn. Members of ACORN and the Working Families Party attempted to bust up the meeting, and security had to restore order. Several people were arrested. New York Public Interest Research Group (NYPIRG) spokesman Gene Russianoff huffed to a reporter that this reform had come "out of nowhere." Of course, that wasn't true. It had come out of a majority vote by New Yorkers for a new mayor who had backed this reform from the start of his campaign. What Russianoff should have said was it hadn't come from the usual sources.

The good-government groups aggressively set the tone for the opposition. They were open, they said, to a thorough examination of the issue. But they asked the commission to withhold putting this election reform measure on the ballot in 2002 because there was insufficient time to study it. Leading the pack was the Citizens Union, the most influential, prestigious, and over-a-century-old good-government group in New York, that had endorsed Bloomberg's election.[31] Its executive director, Linda Stone Davidoff, said, "If the commission proceeds to put it on the ballot, I believe there will be a serious nonpartisan effort throughout the city to reach out to voters and constituents to point out the danger of changing the system."[32]

Democratic Party elected officials, meanwhile, argued that nonpartisan elections were a cynical ploy to dilute the power of minority voters just as they were gaining ascendance within New York City. "Representative Charles B. Rangel, a Manhattan Democrat, who spoke out against the efforts . . . said he might get involved in a campaign to defeat the initiative. 'I hope that it will die on the vine, but if it gets more serious, I may get more serious,' Mr. Rangel said."[33]

Among New York's major dailies, only the *New York Daily News* favored nonpartisan elections. The liberal *New York Times* condemned the measure in two separate editorials, urging the mayor to refrain from putting it before the voters: "New York City, which is overwhelmingly Democratic, has elected two Republican mayors in a row. Whether that shows we're ready for nonpartisan elections or that we manage fine without them is a matter for debate. But minority voters, who are increasingly gaining power in the Democratic Party, may regard nonpartisan elections as just a new way to erode their influence."[34]

On August 25, after two months of public hearings, expert testimony, and a cascade of charges and misinformation about the reform, the CRC voted not to place a measure on the ballot for nonpartisan elections. Many of the commissioners were veterans of the Ed Koch administration, part of New York's Democrat-allied permanent government. All of the commissioners save Kresky voted to table the measure. Kresky submitted a minority report to the commission. "A consensus has been reached to defer placing this matter before the voters. I respect that consensus and trust that over the months to follow our dialogue will continue," Kresky wrote. "Clearly nonpartisan elections is an idea whose time has come—even to New York. I, for one, do not agree with opponents of this reform who argued, 'If it ain't broke, don't fix it.' In my view there is much in our political system that needs fixing."[35]

The Democratic Party, meanwhile, sought to cast it as a defeat for Bloomberg. But the Independence Party elbowed in. Taking responsibility for the loss by not having demonstrated the depth of public support the commission needed to act, the party issued this statement: "The commission's decision is not a defeat for the mayor, whose commitment was simply to establish a process to review the issue. It is, however, a defeat for the Independence Party and for the people of this city." I called all the political reporters in the press room at City Hall with the statement, which they seemed to find comic and baffling. The *Times* covered it the next day with the headline "Party Assigns Itself Blame over Inaction on Charter." "While the idea of pushing nonpartisan elections was criticized by many people around the city, it had the unwavering support of the Independence Party, which yesterday fell on its sword, even though no one in particular asked it to."[36]

Bloomberg was getting a taste of the passion for partisanship within New York City's permanent government circles. But he would not feel the full brunt of their opposition until the following year, when his second Charter Revision Commission voted to put nonpartisan elections on the ballot.

On March 26, 2003, Bloomberg appointed the president of St. Francis College, Frank Macchiarola, a supporter of nonpartisan municipal elections, to lead a new commission. The stage was set for a rematch. At a press conference held in July by a group of Harlem legislators and party leaders to endorse a local politician, Congressman Charles Rangel took the opportunity to try to isolate the mayor. "The only person that I truly know that supports Mayor Bloomberg's position is Lenora Fulani."[37]

In July and August, the Democratic Party kill campaign went into overdrive. Howard Wolfson, who had served as communications director for Hillary Clinton's 2000 Senate campaign and would later join her 2008 presidential campaign (and would go on to work for the 2009 Bloomberg campaign and Bloomberg's third-term administration), coordinated the opposition effort. Democratic Party mayoral hopeful Fernando Ferrer, planning a second run for the mayor's post in 2005, reiterated his opposition to nonpartisan municipal elections on Gabe Pressman's Sunday morning talk show *News Forum*. Ferrer said nonpartisan elections would give candidates the ability "to conceal who they are, to conceal the parties that are supporting them."[38] It was "nothing less than an effort to destroy" the Democratic Party, the liberal *New York Magazine* editorialized.[39]

Every public hearing was attended by elected officials, union officials, and representatives of good-government groups, all of whom condemned nonpartisan municipal elections as an illegitimate reform with no base of support, as a cynical power play by the Republican Bloomberg to undercut minority power, and as an ill-conceived reform that would deny voters—particularly poor voters—vital information about candidates. Their arguments were strangely circular. The elected officials, whose incumbency might be threatened under a nonpartisan system, went on record against the reform. Then the spin doctors argued that the fact that the elected officials opposed it was a sign that nonpartisans were a bad thing. Wolfson said, "The fact that so many of the African-American and Latino elected officials are against this should send a clear signal that it would hurt minority empowerment. . . ."[40] The *New York Times,* reporting on a public hearing on the issue in Queens, wrote, "Elected officials, like the Queens borough president Helen M. Marshall and Democratic Councilman Eric Gioia, spoke passionately for keeping the system as it is." And, its reporter continued, ". . . a growing number of elected officials, like United States Representatives Charles B. Rangel and Jerrold Nadler, have denounced nonpartisan elections on the grounds that they would make it more difficult for minorities to get elected."[41] Even the 2004 presidential candidates got into the act. The *New York Sun,* in the article "Four Presidential Candidates Oppose Nonpartisan Push," noted that presidential candidate Howard Dean sent an email to his New York City networks: "Eliminating primary elections would mean disempowering community-based bodies that work on a grassroots level and provide a starting point for future candidates." And Congressman Dennis Kucinich, through a spokesman, criticized the idea as "harmful to the democratic process," calling it a reform that would aid "with celebrity candidates and billionaire candidates."[42]

The IP battled back, mobilizing hundreds of independents and other community leaders to testify at the hearings. *New York Newsday* reported, "Lt. Eric Adams, president of 100 Blacks in Law Enforcement Who Care [later elected to the State Senate from Brooklyn], said creating nonpartisan elections would allow all New Yorkers to participate in primaries where the top two candidates are selected for the general election. . . . 'They will force the candidates to know the people and not hide behind party labels,' Adams said. . . . 'We have a serious problem in the electoral process and those voters who stay home each election day . . . are sending an indictment for change,' he added."[43] Captain Paul Washington of the Vulcan Society, the fraternal organization of black firefighters, added, "We all know the Democratic machine has almost complete control over who gets elected in New York City. . . . That has got to change."[44] A former chief of the Department of Justice's Voting Rights Division, J. Gerald Hebert, rebutted the arguments that minority voters would be hurt by nonpartisan elections. Addressing the longstanding difficulty in creating cohesive black/Latino coalitions inside the Democratic Party, he explained, "Since blacks and Hispanics do not tend to vote cohesively in such [primary] elections, minority voters do not gain any special advantage or benefits from a partisan primary. Indeed, it has proven an insuperable barrier to their electoral success."[45]

The *Daily News* reiterated its support for the reform in July. "Voters are fed up with the shenanigans. This was evident in the recent Charter Revision Commission hearings, where 80 percent of those who testified spoke in favor of nonpartisan elections. Those in opposition were primarily elected Democratic Party officials. No wonder. Most elections for City Council and other citywide offices are decided in Democratic primaries. The November vote is more often than not pro forma."[46] And then right before the election, two endorsements: John Avlon, in the *New York Sun*, argued, "Nonpartisan elections will empower the 1.2 million New York City voters effectively shut out of the system for selecting candidates. The fastest growing segment of the electorate has the most to gain."[47] The *New York Observer* added, "Corruption and apathy are rotting New York's body politic. Voter turnout is low because voters are smart enough to know that professional politicos have hijacked the electoral process. Mr. Bloomberg wants to give politics back to the voters. He deserves the voters' support."[48]

During the summer Mayor Bloomberg maintained his support, adding provisions to the proposed changes to sweeten the pot for Democrats. Candidates' names could appear on the ballot with a party label, providing "cues" to the voters as to who they were voting for. Any proposed changes to the election system would not go into effect until 2009, after he was out of office—a pledge Bloomberg hoped would persuade the *New York Times* to withdraw its opposition. It didn't work. The good-government groups kept hammering away, offering political science–style analyses of the negative consequences of nonpartisanship. Francis Barry, the mayor's speechwriter and adviser on the nonpartisan campaign, later observed, "Public policy analysis, and especially election analysis, is not a perfect science. Far from it. But in 2003 good-government leaders seemed to believe that by conducting a 'methodologically defensible, empirical analysis,' one will arrive at Truth. In fact, methodologically defensible analyses arrive at different answers as a matter of course."[49] In truth (no pun intended), the Bloomberg team misunderstood the nature of the Democratic Party objections. Party leaders never even considered the merits of the reform. They viewed it as an assault on the citadel. Bloomberg and the Independence Party were the barbarians (actually, he was the billionaire; we were the barbarians) at the gates.

But despite the onslaught, advisers told me that Bloomberg's internal polling was showing support for nonpartisan elections holding steady at around 56 percent. The Macchiarola Commission, unlike its predecessor, voted on August 25, 2003, to place the measure—Question 3—on the ballot. And the battle was joined.

For the Independence Party, the commission's vote was a victory of no small order. New Yorkers were being given the opportunity to back a change in their voting system that would allow one million independents in New York City to share in choosing the finalists who would compete in a general election. But the next phase of the campaign would be exceedingly difficult. The 2003 election cycle, known as an "off year," had no major state or local elections to pull voters to the polls. In addition, all but

2 of 51 city council races had been decided in the primaries because, ironically, under the existing partisan system, in almost
every district the winner of the Democratic primary was the automatic winner in the general election. This meant that the voters inclined to come out on Election Day were not just "prime"
voters[50] but machine voters, loyalists to the party organizations
and their local chieftains. This was not a voting universe friendly
to nonpartisan reform. It was the electoral equivalent of asking
cannibals to vote on whether they should be required to become
vegetarians.

Thus, the fate of Question 3 turned on the capacity of the
Bloomberg-IP alliance to reach and inspire nonpartisan voters—Democrats and Republicans who were not party-liners and
independents—in direct competition with a hardened political
machine with generations of experience in vote-pulling and a far-
flung political infrastructure to boot. The independent movement
was overmatched from the minute the commission took its vote.

The IP had energetic and talented organizers, an embryonic citywide infrastructure, and a deep passion for the issue.
Bloomberg had the resources to put those tools to work. The task
was daunting because there was so little time—only 65 days to the
election. I reached Sheekey and told him my concerns. The positive polling meant nothing in the face of the clubhouse/union/lib-
eral media behemoth. Bloomberg had to spend some significant
money, in some very particular ways, and I wanted to tell him why.
Sheekey set up a meeting.

In mid-September, Stewart and I met up with Sheekey in the driveway at Gracie Mansion.[51] He led us through a back entrance, where we huddled as we told him what we planned to pitch. We threaded our way through a series of narrow passageways (I'm sure it only seemed like a secret tunnel) and then up a quaint wooden staircase into a charming carpeted sitting room with floral wallpaper, rich upholstery, and Dutch-era antiques. He deposited us there as we waited for the mayor.

Shortly, Bloomberg arrived with Cunningham in tow. I told him the issue was simple. We'd come this far. There was a lot at stake. But, I explained, it wasn't just that nonpartisans were on the line. The Independence Party itself was on the line. He was aware that there were powerful forces in the city out to destroy us. They hoped to use the nonpartisan battle to close us down. Many Democrats wanted the Working Families Party, not the Independence Party, to be the kingmaker minor party in New York City politics. They were intent upon shoving us to the margins. We need your help, I told Mike. We need you to ante up for the campaign. We will fight all the way to the finish, because this is our issue. But we need you to have our back.

As I recall, Mike made a few perfunctory remarks about how opponents were trying to tag him as spending to subvert the will of the people. But, he mainly listened. Cunningham was silent, bordering on sulky. He hadn't liked the issue from day one. Mike told us he would think about it, and exited. Sheekey magically reappeared, gave us a quick tour of this restricted floor of Gracie

Mansion, and escorted us out. Stewart and I went to a nearby restaurant, called Newman to tell him about the conversation, and had several very dry martinis.

For three weeks afterward, there was radio silence. Then one afternoon in mid-October my cell phone rang. It was Sheekey. "We're going nuclear!" he told me. I didn't know what that meant, but I figured it had to do with money. Mike was going to spend $7 million on a campaign to pull out a "yes" vote on Question 3. That's great, I told him.

But both the timing and the amount were off. The campaign consisted of truckloads of glossy mailings extolling the virtues of nonpartisan elections. There was no ground game, no television commercials, no mayoral stumping for the issue. The Independence Party, supplied with literature and little else, fielded 500 volunteers on Election Day, while the unions alone put as many as 2,000 workers on the streets to oppose Question 3. The die was cast. The total voter turnout was 11 percent. When the results came in with 31 percent having voted "yes," I was surprised it was so high.

The Democrats were in full gloat. "'Today is the day New Yorkers woke up and found the emperor has no clothes,' said Howard Wolfson, speaking for the state Democratic Party. 'This shows the mayor has no political base, and that will hurt him in 2005.'"[52] The day after the vote, Fernando Ferrer set up an exploratory committee for a mayoral run in 2005.

The mood in the Bloomberg camp was dismal. The mayor made a brief public statement acknowledging the will of the voters, and then, I was told, refused to speak to anyone on his team about the results. I called him anyway, and he called me back. He seemed depressed and battered by how crushing the opposition had been. Years later he told me the campaign had been mismanaged by his team (it was), but he didn't say that on this call. I told him I wasn't depressed, that I was proud of the 145,000 New Yorkers[53] who had stood up to the partisan machine in the face of such an onslaught. These 145,000 people were the base of a new independent reform movement. It was going to take time, work, and money to build that movement, and he had to be in it for the long haul. He thanked me for my efforts, but he was gruff. The Democrats had dealt him a heavy blow. And the press was busy writing his political obituary.

SIX

THE POWER
OF FUSION

AFTER THE ELECTION OF 2000, THE THIRD PARTIES WERE STUCK IN A KIND OF NO man's land. The Federal Election Commission (FEC) required that in order to be recognized as an official national party, its candidate must poll 5 percent of the vote in a presidential election. This would qualify the party for federal funding for its subsequent presidential campaign. Other than John Anderson in 1980 and Ross Perot, who polled 19 percent in 1992 and 8.5 percent in 1996, no independent presidential candidate had managed to meet that benchmark. Though Ralph Nader hoped to deliver that status to the Green Party in 2000, he polled below 3 percent. That year the other national third parties, the Libertarian and the Constitution parties, failed to capture even one half of one percent. For all the appeal that the *idea* of a third party might have, Americans weren't voting for them, especially if they were ideological.

The marginality of the third parties was exacerbated by their ideological and sectarian differences, which prevented them from coalescing in any meaningful way. Other than jointly supporting ballot access reform through coalitions like the Coalition for Fair and Open Elections (COFOE), led by Richard Winger, or debate reform through groups like Rock the Debates, led by Robert Sullentrup and Larry Reinsch, the third parties had no way to combine forces. Acting alone, they nibbled at the margins.

With the third-party movement largely irrelevant while growing numbers of Americans disaligned from the major parties, might there be a way to incentivize the third parties to engage in movement-building together, to join forces for growth? This would mean challenging some of the standard definitions of parties.

A group of 20 independents affiliated with a cross-section of local and national third parties and voter associations agreed to pose such a question to the Federal Election Commission (FEC). In a formal Advisory Opinion Request (AOR) presented in January 2002, the applicants asked whether the FEC would allow presidential funding to be allocated to "a coalition running one or more candidates in the year 2004, who in the aggregate obtain five percent of the vote." The AOR stipulated that the distribution of the funds would be "on the basis of the performance of the various candidates."[1]

Conceived by strategist Fred Newman and assembled by Committee for a Unified Independent Party (CUIP) general counsel Harry Kresky, the AOR set forth a novel and unorthodox argument: that the design of the federal campaign finance system was warping the nascent independent political movement.

By restricting the availability of funding to a particular candidate or a particular party, the independent political movement has been deformed by requiring it to function in a manner which severely limits its growth or to forego funding altogether . . . despite the fact that far more than 5% of the American people identified themselves as independents, these same people were, for the most part, unwilling to vote for the candidate of the several minor or third parties that competed in the 2000 election. . . . Independents will not vote for the candidate of a political party they identify as a smaller version of the two major parties.

It is our belief that in order to realize its full potential for growth, the independent movement must seek the support of the American people as a broad coalition—of parties, activists, networks, movements—committed to opening up the political process and breaking the two-party gridlock. The coalition must, by its very structure, demonstrate that it has moved beyond the partisanship which, particularly post-Florida, is so characteristic of the major parties.

Further, the AOR noted, "An independent political movement characterized by partisan entities whose internal battles and competition with each other appear to be the same partisan mode of behavior associated with the major parties, only on a smaller scale, cannot claim the allegiance of the American people."[2]

Kresky argued that, insofar as funding was necessary for growth, because the Federal Election Campaign Act prescribed the precise form that growth could take, the Constitution was being violated because the federal government had become involved in predetermining forms of political association.

The FEC responded in March, asserting the proposal was "not in accord with either the language or the legislative intent of the Fund Act." Citing the landmark Supreme Court decision *Buckley v. Valeo*, which determined that limits on contributions to political campaigns are constitutional, the FEC said that while third parties needed to be treated fairly, the Fund Act was to "serve the important public interest against providing artificial incentives to splintered parties and unrestrained factionalism." Supporting the Kresky proposal, the FEC said, "would clearly run counter to these concerns."[3]

It was noteworthy that a proposal designed to *overcome* factionalism in the independent political movement was dismissed on the grounds that it would *promote* factionalism. The AOR request hit a dead end.

However marginal the third parties were, the major parties were also undergoing an identity crisis of sorts. Republican power broker and Bush adviser Karl Rove told the *New Yorker* in 2003, "I think we're at a point where the two major parties have sort of exhausted their governing agendas. . . . We had agendas that were originally formed, for the Democrats, in the New Deal, and, for the Republicans, in opposition to the New Deal—modified by the Cold War and further modified by the changes in the sixties, the Great Society and societal and cultural changes. It's sort of like the exhaustion of two boxers fighting it out in the middle of the ring." How do parties die off? Rove had his answer. "Political parties kill themselves or are killed, not by the other political party but by their failure to adapt to new circumstances."[4]

How could independents operate meaningfully in an environment where third parties were at the margins, where each major party was scrambling to dominate the other while adapting to new circumstances, and where a third of the electorate was unaffiliated?

The signs were already pointing against another attempt at independent party building. Arguably, the greatest success in mobilizing independent political power after 2000 had come in the form of "fusion." The Independence Party of New York had used a fusion strategy to elect a nonpartisan mayor. Rather than run its own third-party candidate, it had endorsed Michael Bloomberg, who also ran on the Republican Party line. This enabled the Independence Party, and independent voters, to leverage their political agenda for nonpartisan reform in the mainstream of government and electoral politics. In this case, the Independence Party's support had been crucial to Bloomberg's victory. Though fusion, or cross-endorsement by minor parties, is banned in all but six states, the willingness of independents to "play the field" politically speaking meant that fusion strategies could be deployed without a political party, simply through independents organizing and engaging politically.

At a national conference of 400 independent activists from 37 states, titled "The Power of Fusion," Fred Newman encouraged the movement to adopt a fusion strategy. Being independent did not automatically mean having to vote for an independent, he argued. That was as partisan as the Republicans or Democrats requiring party loyalty. Independents could choose to support candidates based on whether they advanced their cause, no matter the label. Building at the base was key. "That's what fusion means," he said. "That's what fusion power is. And we can accomplish this. We can't wait to participate as players until we win the reforms we're talking about. We have to participate as players right now, and that can be done."[5]

That fusion approach was used to frame a new strategy for organizing independents to engage in presidential politics. This strategy became known by its acronym, "ChIP," for Choosing an Independent President.

During 2003, ChIP reached out to presidential candidates of all stripes—Democrat, Republican, and independent. It challenged every contender to establish a connection to independent voters by going through the ChIP process. An 11-part questionnaire for presidential candidates was developed as a gateway to the conversation.[6]

Among the 2004 Democratic contenders who participated in ChIP (Howard Dean, John Edwards, Dennis Kucinich, Al

Sharpton),[7] the most engaged was Howard Dean. The Dean movement was stirring the Democratic Party from its defeatist torpor. ChIP's national polling showed that the strongest prospect to "Beat Bush" was Dean with support from independents, many of whom were beginning to turn against the war in Iraq. Dean entered the ChIP process by submitting his questionnaire in July 2003.

In early October in California, Governor Dean met with Jim Mangia, one of ChIP's conveners. Dean told Mangia that he believed he could "remake the Democratic Party" through his campaign. Mangia indicated that independents might be interested in supporting him, so long as they were not asked to give up their identity as independents in the process. That, he explained, was the purpose of ChIP. A serious coalition of independents and Dean Democrats could not only beat Bush, it could dramatically curtail right-wing influence in American politics.

Mangia also underscored to Dean that Democratic Party attacks on Ralph Nader and Nader voters had soured independents on such a coalition, but that he could overcome that—and in doing so, remove the impetus for a Nader or Nader-style candidacy. Mangia, meanwhile, had been trying to persuade Nader that if he were to decide to run for president again in 2004, he should use his candidacy to unite the independent movement by running as a coalition candidate, not as the candidate of a single party as he had done in 2000.

Dean's star continued to rise as he forcefully criticized the war in Iraq. ChIP pressed the cause of the independent voter with him (and with Edwards, Kucinich, Sharpton, and Wesley Clark), feeding Dean opportunities to distinguish himself as an advocate for the empowerment of independents.

A CNN debate in Arizona in October put a spotlight on that state's primary. In 1988 Arizona voters had passed a referendum opening party primaries to include the state's half a million independent voters. However, Arizona Attorney General Janet Napolitano then ruled that the initiative did not apply to presidential primaries. ChIP asked Dean to call on the Arizona Democratic Party to open its presidential primary to include independents. Meanwhile, ChIP mobilized independents to pressure CNN to ask the presidential candidates a question about independent voters. Debate host Judy Woodruff framed the question in terms of the voter revolt that had occurred two days prior to the debate in the California recall vote and the election of Arnold Schwarzenegger. Exit polls showed that independents voted by a margin of 56 percent to 44 percent in favor of recalling Governor Gray Davis. No one, including Dean, picked up on the role of the independent voter in that revolt.[8]

Throughout the early fall, ChIP's conversation with Dean remained at arm's length, until the campaign to adopt nonpartisan elections in New York City reached a boiling point. This coincided with a series of visits by Democratic primary contenders to the Big Apple.

In the ChIP questionnaire, Dean had pledged his support for nonpartisan municipal elections. However, in 2003, the New York

City Democratic Party machine was in the midst of a feverish campaign to block them. New Yorkers were about to go to the polls to vote on Question 3, the Bloomberg/Independence initiative. As Election Day approached, Democratic Party operatives dug deep for every ounce of meaningful opposition they could muster. A week before the election, a letter from Governor Dean urging voters to come out to defeat nonpartisan elections was rushed into circulation.

The Dean flip-flop caught the attention of the New York media. The *New York Post* reported: "Democratic presidential challenger Howard Dean came out swinging against nonpartisan elections yesterday and accused Mayor Bloomberg of trying to change the rules to benefit the rich. . . . Dean had some explaining to do after a recent questionnaire surfaced in which he supported nonpartisan elections."[9] The *Daily News* weighed in, too: "Democratic presidential hopeful Howard Dean's foray into New York City politics backfired yesterday when he appeared to take conflicting positions on whether party primaries for local offices should be dumped."[10]

That night the Dean campaign staff reached out to me. Dean's New York campaign, run by insider Democrats, had pressed for the statement, they said. The national campaign had given way. Dean's staff—at least the ones I spoke to—were unhappy. They'd been caught in a squeeze between independent reformers and a local Democratic machine. A staffer later told me that day became known around Dean's national campaign headquarters as "Black Monday."

Dean was fighting to gain mainstream acceptance for his candidacy. When he received the endorsement of former Vice President Al Gore, it appeared he was making inroads into the Democratic establishment. But this also heightened the anxiety among Dean's core supporters. One staffer told me that the Gore endorsement did not mean that they were going "inside." Rather, he said, they would remain as "outside" as they had ever been.

On December 13, 2003, Saddam Hussein was captured by U.S. military forces in Iraq, a major breakthrough on the war front. Dean observed, "The capture of Saddam is a good thing which I hope very much will keep our soldiers in Iraq and around the world safer. . . . But the capture of Saddam has not made America safer."[11] Dean's remark, an explicit critique of the Bush war policy, unnerved the Democratic establishment. They felt he had gone too far. The war against Dean began to escalate.

Under heavy fire from his Democratic primary opponents, Dean began to slip in the polls. Reporters, pundits, and party officials opined that the capture of Saddam might prove the undoing of Dean, because it boosted Bush's credibility and undermined the argument against the war. Meanwhile, Dean seemed blinded by his front-runner status. Worse still, he was blind to the lengths his own party would go to destroy him as soon as they sensed he was vulnerable. Major Democratic donors were recruited to efforts to erode his credibility.

Meanwhile, ChIP pressed Dean to appear at its New Hampshire conference, set for early January, urging him to use it as a national platform to reinforce his political independence and pursue a "Beat Bush" coalition with the independent voter. But the Dean campaign was trapped in a downward spiral. He committed everything to winning in Iowa and New Hampshire, spending $40 million and all of his political capital on salvaging his candidacy. The ChIP negotiations with the Dean campaign continued until 48 hours before its New Hampshire event. At one point U.S. Senator Jim Jeffords, a former Republican-turned-independent, was proposed as a stand-in for Dean. Despite an impressive show of strength, Dean lost the Iowa caucuses on January 19, 2004. As soon as he gave his post-Iowa "I Have a Scream" speech, the Democrats buried him. The gathering of 300 independent voters and opinionmakers in Bedford, New Hampshire, went forward without him.

As Dean's star faded, Ralph Nader was waiting in the wings. He had been watching the Democrats' pressure on Dean, their search for an "electable" candidate—John Kerry—and the opening he believed that Dean's exit created for an antiwar independent. Nader contacted Mangia and told him he wanted to attend ChIP's conference in New Hampshire.

Nader was well received by the ChIP delegates, though his remarks focused primarily on ballot access issues. He did not present himself as a candidate, but he did argue that Gore's loss to George Bush in 2000 was not a function of votes he took from Gore. "There's huge arrogance in that statement, too. It's as if Al Gore is entitled to the votes of people who didn't want to vote for him," Nader told the delegates.

After the meeting, Nader and his campaign manager, Theresa Amato, sat down with Mangia, Newman, and me in a freezing-cold conference room. The discussion was brief. Were he to run, he told us, he planned to run coalitionally and not ally with any single party, in essence following the plan Mangia had given him two years earlier. There was some discussion about the sectarianism of the third parties, particularly those on the left. Nader seemed confident he could overcome it. He asked for our support should he decide to run.

Six weeks later, the day before Nader went on *Meet the Press* to announce his intention to run again, Newman sent Nader a note urging him not to run, but pledging his full support if he made the decision to go. "You and you alone have the power to galvanize that [independent] movement during what will be a farce of a presidential campaign," Newman wrote. "If you are a candidate I fear you will be pigeonholed, not simply as a spoiler but as a 'quack.' That will become the story, and your call for greater democracy and leveling the political playing field to challenge the bipartisan monopoly will be obscured."

Further, Newman wrote, "I've always insisted that I discipline myself to choose fights carefully. I'm a million percent behind the one you want to have. But, in my view, this is not the moment to have it." Newman urged Nader to spend the presidential campaign not as a candidate but, instead, as a champion for the independent movement. "The response to ChIP tells me there is traction at the base for this nontraditional approach."[12]

Nader went ahead with his run anyway. The ChIP networks supported him. Newman and Cathy Stewart worked with the Independence Party's state chairman to secure its line on New York's ballot for Nader that year, on which he polled 100,000 votes, or nearly 25 percent of his total vote nationally. Wayne Griffin, chairman of the South Carolina Independence Party and a leader in the ChIP process, also put Nader on his state's ticket.

The remnants of the Reform Party—which consisted of four ballot lines in Colorado, Kansas, Mississippi, and Montana—backed Nader, too. The Green Party rejected the coalition and backed their own candidate, David Cobb, in their "safe states" strategy. They ran Cobb only in states that were so firmly "red" or "blue" that the Green vote could not possibly impact the outcome.

The Democrats, meanwhile, aggressively tried to throw Nader off the ballot, challenging him in some 21 states. Theresa Amato noted poignantly, "right then and there, I felt the entire decay of the Democratic Party in the United States. They were going to win by bullying to make sure no third party or independent could run against them or no voter could have any other choice. I was ashamed for them. Saddened."[13]

The left-wing media played their usual role of protecting the Democratic Party and demonizing the independents. The most vituperative attack came from Christopher Hitchens in *Vanity Fair*. Hitchens hated everything about the campaign. He hated that Nader was running. He hated that he was working with Newman and Fulani who, according to Hitchens, were (a) fascists,

(b) zombies, (c) cultists, and probably worst of all (d) had backed Mike Bloomberg. Sometimes the political world gets so crazy, you just have to laugh. The closing event of the campaign was a visit to Harlem, where Fulani organized an audience of 400 at the Emmanuel AME Church to hear Nader speak.

George Bush won reelection. Nader polled 463,653 votes. The Greens got 119,859 votes. Independent voters overall split 48–49 for Bush and Kerry. The presidential race came down to Ohio, which Bush narrowly carried. Independent voters, who made up 25 percent of the Ohio electorate, split 40 percent for Bush and 59 percent for Kerry. The total vote for all independent presidential candidates was 1,226,291, or about 1 percent. The independent movement had passed through the 2004 presidential election without leaving a footprint.

SEVEN

BLOOMBERG'S DILEMMA, PART 2

IN THE SUMMER OF 2004, AGAINST THE BACKDROP OF A PRESIDENTIAL CAMPAIGN that had begun with a surge of anti–Iraq War fervor behind Howard Dean but sputtered into a contest between the electable John Kerry and the incumbent George W. Bush, in which independent voters and candidates played a largely negligible role, Mike Bloomberg and his team began to lay the groundwork for a 2005 reelection bid. By June Bloomberg's approval rating had climbed back up to 50 percent. But some polls still showed him losing a reelection bid to Democrat Fernando Ferrer by six points.[1]

In the middle of July, at an early morning strategy meeting at Bloomberg's home on the Upper East Side, the earliest plans were discussed. Kevin Sheekey brought me to the meeting, a signal that the Independence Party would be positioned as a more major partner in this second run. Deputy Mayor Patti Harris and pollster

Doug Schoen were also there. There was a beautifully laid continental breakfast, complete with croissants and coffee. While we waited for Mike, Harris and I chatted. Aware that I was the outsider in the group, she tried to put me at ease.

When Mike joined us, Schoen ran through his latest polling, which showed an upward bump in the mayor's popularity. "You obviously didn't include Diana, then," Bloomberg quipped, referencing a private spat between him and his companion Diana Taylor at a public event, which had just been reported in the papers. We all laughed.

Soon the conversation turned to the fundamentals of the reelection campaign. Everyone in the room believed that the Democratic nominee would be Fernando Ferrer, who had been edged out by Mark Green in the 2001 run-off. The mayor was cautious about the impact a Ferrer candidacy would have on the dynamics of the race. Given Ferrer's ethnicity, he would dominate the Latino vote. And, Bloomberg thought, the 25 percent of the black vote he had attracted in 2001 would not repeat. That vote had been entirely situational, he said. Black voters were angry at Mark Green for the Sharpton leaflet affair. Everyone agreed that level of black support would not hold. Except me.

I did not think the black vote for Bloomberg in 2001 was simply a revenge vote. The New York Democratic Party's relationship to black voters was strained. Lenora Fulani and other black leaders had harnessed some of that sentiment at postelection community meetings, where they encouraged African Americans to be more independent. New polls by the Joint Center for Political and Economic Studies showed that 34 percent of African Americans between 18 and 25 considered themselves independents, not Democrats.[2] The Independence Party's base in Harlem and predominantly black communities in Brooklyn and Queens was growing substantially. If Bloomberg were to encourage that—if he were to reach out more strongly using his connection to the Independence Party (IP) to further brand himself as independent of both major parties (in 2004 he was still a registered Republican)—I argued, we could sustain and expand his coalition with black voters.

To say the response in the room was chilly would be an understatement. Sheekey, Schoen, and Harris were all Democrats. Even Bloomberg had been a Democrat before he became a Republican to avoid a crowded primary field in 2001. They wanted to beat the Democratic Party nominee in 2005, certainly. But no one, other than me, was interested in upsetting the Democratic Party's hegemony in the black community. Suffice it to say, this was the last "inner circle" meeting at Bloomberg's home that I was invited to attend. But, in 2005, the black community proved me right. History doesn't always listen to the inner circle.

The bottom line was that Bloomberg needed and wanted the Independence Party line. For independents, Bloomberg was a powerful ally who could continue to advance the cause of nonpartisan reform. Sheekey and I discussed the importance of investing in independent infrastructure-building for the campaign. The lessons of the Question 3 loss were still fresh. The tension, though, was over the question of who would "own" that infrastructure. I wanted Mike to invest in building the Independence Party infrastructure—in effect, to become a partner with us in expanding the party's on-the-ground capability to serve as the base of a new reform movement in New York. The Bloomberg team was ready to do more basebuilding. But they wanted to control what they built.

Still, they recognized that the stronger the IP was, the more it could benefit them. And so Sheekey counteroffered by proposing that pollster Doug Schoen conduct a "census" of the IP membership, which would allow us to expand our contact with the party's members in New York City.

The census produced some interesting and—for the Bloomberg team—unexpected results. A ten-question "drill down" to 60,000 of the IP's 80,000 New York City members established that the party's outspoken advocacy for nonpartisan reform made it very popular with its base, and that insofar as Bloomberg was identified as partnering with the IP for a reform agenda, his popularity among independents notably increased. When he saw the results, Fred Newman told Cathy Stewart, "Looks like they told 'em what you taught them to say!"

Schoen's survey was notable for establishing statistically what organizers of independents had known for some time. Political reform was an issue that animated independents. Sixty-six percent believed electoral reform was needed. Among independents who wanted to become active in the movement, 86 percent believed electoral reform was vital. On the day that Schoen presented the results to Stewart and me, he was more enthusiastic than I'd ever seen him. It was kind of a holy-grail moment. Through the census, Schoen saw clearly what we'd been organizing on the ground for more than a decade.

Bloomberg's official campaign to seek the Independence Party nomination for his reelection bid kicked off on December 6, 2004. Mike gave a keynote address at the Independence Party's annual fund-raiser, the Anti-Corruption Awards, which took place in the usual hail of controversy. Democratic politicians started complaining about Bloomberg's plan to attend days before the event took place. Mayoral spokesman Ed Skyler told the New York Post, "The Independence Party recognized long ago that our political system needs real reform and the mayor is proud to stand with them."[3] The day before the event, City Council Speaker Gifford Miller released to the press a letter to Bloomberg, calling on him to renounce the Independence Party and its line. When contacted by reporters, I reminded them that Miller himself had run on the Independence Party line in 1997. Bloomberg communications director Bill Cunningham told the press that Miller had "selective amnesia."[4] The IP's press secretary, Sarah Lyons, was so miffed at the media's determination to drive a wedge that she put them all behind a velvet rope and refused to let them circulate in the 400-person crowd at the event. When Sheekey arrived with the mayor, the press corps begged him, from behind the rope, to let them out. Sheekey good humoredly asked if we could "liberate" the reporters. I agreed, much to Lyons's chagrin.

Bloomberg delivered a strong message that night: he wanted to reconstitute his winning coalition in 2005, in spite of pressure from Miller and other Democrats to do otherwise.

To all the critics who are rushing to criticize me for being here tonight, let me point out that this night is about the 1 million New Yorkers who are denied the most basic right by the two major political parties. And if the two major political parties were willing to take on the status quo and reduce their own power, then none of us would be standing in this room and we could be holiday shopping. Enough.

There's a word for what happens when election laws prevent a large section of the population from fully participating in the democratic process. It's called disenfranchisement, and that's why we're here. The poll tax is the most obvious form of disenfranchising voters. But other election laws can have the same effect, and the situation is particularly bad here in New York because many independents are young people and many are immigrants. They are the future of democracy and they are being shut out of elections. And that's why I supported nonpartisan elections along with the Independence Party, because we believe that every single voter should be treated equally and that's what the party bosses don't want to have happen. Let's be honest about what this is all about. It's taking away their power, their ability to control the electorate, their ability to disenfranchise anyone who would vote against them, who wouldn't do exactly what they're told to do. . . .

We all know that election reform takes time. That's because those who have benefited from the system are the ones who fight hardest to preserve it. So if we're going to succeed, we're going to need an independent coalition of citizens who believe in reform, who believe that our election laws should treat everyone equally, who believe that low levels of competition and participation are not healthy for democracy.

The Independence Party is helping to build that coalition and I'm happy to join you in doing so.

The audience cheered him. And the press revived their questions about the partnership. "The courting of the Independence Party line represents a somewhat odd alliance for Mr. Bloomberg," wrote Jennifer Steinhauer of the *New York Times*, the day after the event. "The mayor is fond of saying that he makes no decision for political reasons alone, and usually refrains from attaching himself to controversial or overly ideological causes."[5] Shortly afterward, Bloomberg made a $250,000 gift to the city party.

Meanwhile, building on the rising tide of independence in the minority communities, Fulani set out to assemble what she called the "Bloomberg on C" coalition, a network of black and Latino community leaders—mainly Democrats—who would champion voting for the mayor on the Independence Party's crucial Column C line. These activists—a mix of clergy, small business owners, educators, police and corrections officers, sanitation workers, Democratic district leaders—coalesced around two ideas. First, that the mayor deserved reelection. And second, that voting for Bloomberg as an independent gave the communities of color a new source of leverage. Voting for Bloomberg on Column C made a statement, not just about the independence of the candidate, but about the independence of the voter.

As the Bloomberg on C effort began to take root, the central Bloomberg campaign began its own survey of hundreds of thousands of New York voters, creating a behemoth database based on a novel set of postmodern meta-categories that supplanted typical race- and neighborhood-based models.[6] Bloomberg's strategists were, in their own way, doing battle with traditional identity politics. In the course of these surveys, they discovered that Bloomberg was appealing to a cross-section of black voters on a significant scale. The bottom-up persuasion efforts of the Bloomberg on C coalition were starting to register.

The Bloomberg team adjusted its game plan, bringing on black advisers with links to the Harlem machine.[7] A press conference launching "African Americans for Bloomberg" featured high-profile black celebrities, such as restauranteur B. Smith and fashion model Iman. Basketball great Magic Johnson came on board, too. These were not political heavyweights—in fact, most of them weren't even city voters. Nonetheless, the Bloomberg campaign had come around to believing that the black vote was in play.

The first public measure of the depth of support Bloomberg was enjoying among black voters came in a shocking Marist poll two weeks after Fernando Ferrer won the September Democratic primary. The Marist survey showed that 50 percent of black voters were planning to vote for Bloomberg.[8] Some Bloomberg advisers simply did not believe the numbers. "From your lips to God's ears," one of them told me. But they did feel confident enough in their black support to decline having the mayor participate in a televised debate at the Apollo Theatre in Harlem in early October, sponsored by the local cable news network, NY1. The mayor was not a great debater, and NY1 was known to be hostile to him. Mortified by the Marist poll, black Democrats struck back. Al Sharpton, who had kept a low profile during most of the campaign, criticized Bloomberg's decision to skip the debate as a sign of disrespect for the black community.

The Bloomberg on C coalition turned up the heat. Staging a large informational picket outside the Apollo on the night of the debate were Fulani, prominent Democratic district leaders Lisa Kenner and Theresa Freeman, educator Barbara Taylor, Bob McCullough, the president of Each One Teach One, attorney Alvaader Frazier, union activist Michael Hall, Imam Charles Bilal, and scores of others. They emphatically endorsed the electoral revolution underway in the black community. A few days after the Apollo debate, a new set of polls showed Bloomberg's support among black voters holding at 53 percent, with 75 percent saying that Sharpton's endorsement of Bloomberg's opponent, Fernando Ferrer, made little difference to them one way or the other.[9]

On Election Day, the Independence Party and the Bloomberg on C coalition fielded a vote-pulling operation in various neighborhoods. In black community districts where volunteers worked, up to a third of Bloomberg's vote was cast on Column C. Citywide, one out of every eight black voters pulled the Column C lever. Overall, Bloomberg polled an astounding 47 percent of the black vote. The Independence vote totals jumped dramatically in white liberal areas like Park Slope and Manhattan's Upper East Side. And in a mark of the IP's signature, nonideological brand, it also attracted voters from conservative Staten Island and parts of Queens.

Bloomberg scored an overwhelming victory in 2005. He won by 250,000 votes and further established his national reputation as a nonpartisan mayor. The Independence Party vote was 75,000, a 22 percent increase from the 2001 vote of 59,000 and 6 percent of the total votes cast. Meanwhile, the vote totals on the Democratic and Republican lines went down.

But for all the jubilation over the victory, the evident growth of the Independence Party, and the black-led electoral revolution against the Democratic Party, there was trouble ahead. Powerful New York Democratic Party leaders, including Senator Hillary Clinton and State Attorney General Eliot Spitzer, who was planning a run for governor, were plainly disconcerted by the 2005 results. They did not have a particular problem with Bloomberg. But the fact that the Independence Party in New York City was led by a circle of progressives with the capacity to disrupt long-held Democratic alignments, with the backing of a billionaire mayor, was becoming less and less tolerable.

Back in the spring, as the 2005 reelection campaign was getting underway, Bloomberg had appeared as a featured speaker at the annual Lincoln Center gala for the All Stars Project, a nonprofit youth development program founded by Newman and Fulani. Congressman Charles Rangel and Harvard professor Henry Louis Gates, Jr., the latter an All Stars board member, joined Bloomberg at the glittering charity event, including a private reception hosted by Newman. Privately funded by a donor base of thousands in the business and philanthropic community (though not by Bloomberg himself), the gala marked the ascendance of this unorthodox circle of progressives. Bloomberg was introduced by All Stars's president, Gabrielle Kurlander, and enthusiastically received by the audience. Two All Stars youth performed a rap dedicated to the mayor, grabbing his hands and holding them aloft in a kind of hip-hop-style victory march around the stage.

Two days after the gala, Fulani was invited to appear on NY1, ostensibly to talk about the event. Instead, interviewer Dominic Carter asked Fulani about a line she had written 16 years earlier in a theater review of a Newman play, *No Room for Zion*, in which she commented on the ways in which Jewish people internationally had been turned against people of color.[10] Carter asserted the comment was anti-Jewish; Fulani disagreed.

Soon NY1 was broadcasting this segment of the interview every 30 minutes. An array of politicians, including Bloomberg, issued statements condemning Fulani's 16-year-old comment. Some called on the IP to repudiate her. The party refused, declaring that it did not take positions on international matters and that party members were free to hold their own views. Fulani declined further comment, feeling that the environment was too overheated for a serious dialogue and that nothing good could come of it.[11]

Several years later, in 2008, she repudiated the controversial lines from her theater review at a press conference at City Hall.[12] But throughout the remainder of 2005 and 2006, the controversy continued, kept alive by Democratic Party leaders who were by then intent on surgically removing the New York City leadership from the Independence Party. Clinton and Spitzer, both privately and publicly, instructed the IP's state chairman Frank MacKay that they would not run on the IP line in 2006 if Fulani and her allies were in leadership positions. The IP's renewal of ballot status was tied to the 2006 governor's race (in which Spitzer was a candidate), so their forfeiture could have implications for the party's continued existence, including its coveted position in Column C. Under this pressure, MacKay removed Fulani and six allies from the executive committee, leaving it without black, Jewish, or city-based members. But even this was insufficient for the critics. MacKay began to systematically dismantle the rules that had established local control of party business, the same rules he and the New York City leaders had crafted when the Democracy Coalition took over the party in 2000. All power would now be concentrated in his hands. He proceeded to bring charges of disloyalty against 130 members of the Independence Party of New York City (IPNYC) and moved to expel them from the party. Cathy Stewart, who had effectively shared leadership of the state party with MacKay, was one of those charged, along with Fulani, Newman, Kresky, and me, and scores of the city party's most active and influential county and citywide leaders.

However, court approval is required to finalize an expulsion, and after a protracted court battle, State Supreme Court Judge Emily Jane Goodman in Manhattan and State Supreme Court Judge Joseph Levine in Brooklyn both ruled that the disenrollments could not be carried out. In her decision, Goodman stated that "there is no evidence whatsoever of their being out of sympathy with the principles of the Party" and that MacKay's motive "appears to be more political than philosophical."[13]

In the early days of this onslaught, Sheekey and I met for coffee at the Bryant Park Grill. I filled him in on the multiple ways that the New York City Independence Party was under attack and the unfounded demonization of Fulani. He took it all in, seeming to weigh the political calculus. So, he said, somewhat sympathetically after I'd laid out the whole picture, they're going to crucify Lenora and we're going to stand by and let it happen. I looked at him, surprised at his candor. That's up to you, I remember saying.

Sheekey and I met again soon after the 2005 reelection campaign. I'd written a memorandum to him and Bloomberg analyzing the election results, encouraging them to move ahead with nonpartisan reform given the mandate of the election. As I recall, he was excited about the prospects for what could be accomplished in the second term. But the pressure from the Democratic elites was just beginning, and MacKay's campaign to wrest control of the city IP organization had yet to play out in the 17 court cases that followed. The mayor, agitated, told me in the days after the 2005 election that Clinton, Spitzer, and Senator Charles Schumer would have nothing to do with us. "We're not in a partnership with them," I told him. "We're in a partnership with you."

With the 2005 reelection wrapped up, and the pressure on the New York City branch of the Independence Party (IPNYC) ramping up, the Bloomberg team began to reorient its relationship to the Independence Party. The mayor was going into his second and final (or so everyone then thought) term in City Hall. He was popular with Democratic voters and, to a large degree, with the Democratic establishment. His approval ratings were in the neighborhood of 70 percent for the first half of 2006.[14]

Bloomberg's inner circle, most notably Sheekey, now wanted distance from their independent New York City allies, who were coming under withering attack from Independence Party state chairman Frank MacKay, in spite of—or, actually because of—the IP's high performance for Bloomberg in the 2005 election. The 75,000 votes on the Independence Party line and 47 percent of the black vote were especially conspicuous in light of the scathing *New York Times* editorial published three days before the election. Decrying the idea that, "The Independence Party is one of the New York third parties that exist by endorsing candidates from other parties who like the idea of another spot on the ballot," the *Times* opened its editorial with this: "Perhaps we should start at the bottom line. Don't vote for any candidates on the Independence Party row in Tuesday's elections."[15]

At the end of 2005, NY1 anchor Dominic Carter, whose interview with Fulani and subsequent six-part "investigative" series on Fred Newman had inflamed the 2005 controversy, pointedly asked Sheekey whether the partnership with the IP had been worth it. Sheekey answered ". . . to write off tens of thousands of New Yorkers who are focused in one party about reforming elections, which the Independence Party is uniquely focused on, is really to diminish them. And Mayor Bloomberg as an independent has always focused on the idea of reforming elections. We have a system now that is not nonpartisan, it's bipartisan. . . . One of the ideas the mayor has always pushed is reforming the electoral system, empowering people who aren't part of the political system."[16]

Bloomberg was an independent in his outlook and his governing style, and Sheekey among others recognized that the more Bloomberg cultivated his image as an independent, the more distinctive and influential he could become in national politics. At the end of 2006, political reporter John Heilemann wrote a cover story for *New York Magazine* floating the idea of an independent presidential bid by Bloomberg.[17] Around that time, I ran into Sheekey at a restaurant near Lincoln Center, and we spent some time talking about this scenario. He asked me to put together notes on how to set up for a national independent campaign, which I sent to both him and Bloomberg. We had not been in contact for nearly a year, as Sheekey had effectively switched sides in the IP internal battle, cultivating his relationship to MacKay. For his part, Bloomberg was friendly, even personal, when city leaders of the party ran into him in public. But he had ignored requests to aid the New York City branch against MacKay's efforts to "cleanse" the party and eviscerate local control. The fact that the nonpartisan election issue was dead and that he would never need the IP line again certainly diminished our leverage with him.

However, when the All Stars sought to refinance the Bloomberg-approved IDA bonds it had used to purchase its 30,000-square-foot national headquarters on West 42nd Street, the mayor fought off a partisan attack on the refinancing proposal. The package would help the All Stars upgrade its youth development center, home to programs that served tens of thousands of inner city kids. It required the approval of the IDA (Industrial Development Agency). Manhattan Borough President Scott Stringer, a Democrat, called a press conference to pressure the IDA to reject the application. Bloomberg's appointees voted to approve the bond at a tense and high-profile IDA board meeting, and the refinancing went through. Questioned about this at a City Hall press conference, Bloomberg defended the vote. "I don't think I heard one argument made that there was something wrong with the All Stars Project, and that's what we look at. We're not going to hurt the kids at the All Stars Project."[18] Bloomberg might have been unwilling to go up against the Clinton-Spitzer-Schumer blockade of the Independence Party's city leadership, but he wouldn't allow local Democrats to politicize the city's support for a popular and effective youth development program.

By the spring of 2007 speculation was rife that Bloomberg might make a run for the presidency. I'd never heard back from Sheekey in response to the requested memorandum, but I had heard through the grapevine that he and MacKay were becoming political buddies, while the IPNYC was battling in court to stop the expulsions and to preserve some modicum of rank-and-file democracy inside the party. In 2006 Cathy Stewart ran a grass-roots drive to create county committees in New York City—the only legally recognized instruments of local control that could not be undone by MacKay's slash-and-burn rules changes that gave all decision-making power to the state executive committee. Stewart's drive involved recruiting, nominating, and campaigning for 4,000 party members who joined the county committees in all five boroughs, a complex and challenging feat she ran with Robert Conroy, the Brooklyn county chair. There was an attempt to disrupt those local elections with forged petitions and fraudulent challenges (the signers' names and addresses were fake), the source of which was never established. These false filings meant that hundreds of primaries for county committee positions were held. Stewart and her team swept the elections, and four local governing committees were certified.[19]

The more Sheekey allied Bloomberg with MacKay while MacKay was attempting to demolish the city organization and expel the party's black, Jewish, and progressive leadership, the more its membership felt that Bloomberg had betrayed them. The fact that in 2008 Bloomberg donated $1.35 million to MacKay's state party account didn't help.[20]

Even though he reregistered as an unaffiliated independent in June 2007, which stimulated a fresh round of speculation about his White House aspirations, the national independent movement was equally suspicious about Bloomberg's modus operandi. In the summer of 2007, CNN asked me whether Bloomberg would be an automatic favorite among independent voters. On *The Situation Room* I told reporter Jim Acosta, "I don't know that that's necessarily the case. . . . Is a Barack Obama, is a John Edwards going to reach out and say, 'Hey, we're about building a new kind of coalition that's going to go up against the establishment'? That's a big question on the table and I think frankly that Mike is a little bit behind the curve right now."[21]

As the presidential speculation grew, MacKay began to appear in the press as a booster for the mayor, positioned as his unofficial link to the organized independent movement. By January 2008, with Hillary Clinton, Barack Obama, John Edwards, Dennis Kucinich, John McCain, Mitt Romney, Mike Huckabee, and others making their way to Iowa, New Hampshire, and South Carolina, MacKay was promoting himself (with Sheekey's blessing) as the independent movement's arbiter of Bloomberg's independent run. "Since September, MacKay says he has driven to 35 states and dropped 35 pounds along the way," reported *New York Newsday*.

"His mission is to stitch together a patchwork of ragtag reform, independent and enviro-third parties to try to clear the way to the ballot for a potential Bloomberg presidential run."[22] MacKay told *Newsday*, "What we're doing is laying the groundwork and we'll get him three quarters of the way there with volunteers."[23] It was MacKay's job to add a patina of grassroots legitimacy to Bloomberg's presidential aspirations.

Ultimately Bloomberg's presidential run came to naught. Though MacKay and Unity08's founders, Doug Bailey and Gerald Rafshoon, had signed on to the bid,[24] ostensibly representing a cross-section of independent movement leaders, both the bid and their "movement" were dead on arrival.

In a *New York Times* editorial in February 2008, Bloomberg announced that he would not run for president in 2008. "These forces that prevent meaningful progress are powerful, and they exist in both parties. I believe that the candidate who recognizes that the party is over—and begins enlisting all of us to clean up the mess—will be the winner this November, and will lead our country to a great and boundless future."[25] While independents across the country flocked to the Obama candidacy, MacKay and the state leadership of the IP endorsed John McCain. Bloomberg chose not to endorse a candidate. Obama went on, with the support of the national networks of IndependentVoting.org,[26] to win 60 percent of independent voters, roughly the same percent of independents that Bloomberg had carried in his 2005 mayoral run. For both Obama and Bloomberg, black voters and independent voters had been key. Historian Omar Ali notes in his book *In the Balance of Power*, "These Americans have become part of a discernible movement linking African Americans with white independents—a black and independent alliance."[27]

In September 2007, while Sheekey and MacKay were still playing footsie with the faux presidential run, the court battles between MacKay and the city's Independence Party came to a dramatic conclusion. Blocked from expelling the 130 targets and unable to undercut the city party's base of 5,000 county committee members and activists, MacKay still managed to rescind every form of local control that the Democracy Coalition had fought to achieve eight years earlier. This included control of IP nominations for local office in the city. Only one caveat evaded his grasp. New York State law explicitly gives the power to make nominations for citywide office to a joint meeting of the five county committees in New York City. Though MacKay attempted to persuade the court that the rule change by the state party which gave him decision-making power over these nominations should take precedence over state law, invoking the constitutional authority of political parties to govern their internal affairs, the IPNYC prevailed. On June 10, 2008, a court of appeals decision affirmed the power of the New York City wing of the party to nominate its mayoral and other citywide candidates in all future elections. The IP's bottom-up progressives had weathered the storm and had managed to grow their support at the base while doing so. From this point on, the city party would operate entirely separately from the state party and would champion the cause of nonpartisan reform alone.

Meanwhile, despite having curtailed his presidential ambitions, Bloomberg was not eager to leave the political stage. The onset of the financial crisis in the fall of 2008 gave him an opening. Together with the Democratic Party–run City Council, he cut a deal to overturn the city's voter-enacted term limits law. When Bloomberg announced in October 2008 that he would seek a third term in office, the City Council voted to allow elected officials to serve three (instead of the original law's two) consecutive terms in office. A public uproar ensued. Bloomberg signed the bill into law.

The Independence Party, allied with Bloomberg on nonpartisan reform for so many years, joined those opposing the change in the term limits law. It filed an amicus brief to a lawsuit seeking to nullify the council vote on the grounds that term limits, having been enacted by two ballot initiatives, could not be repealed except by a ballot initiative. But the suit and the appeal lost. Bloomberg would run for a third term.

His road to reelection would be challenging. Nationally, independent voters had just sent a new postpartisan president to the White House. The spirit in the country—including New York City— was for change, reform, and political independence. Bloomberg, though an independent, had several strikes against him. He had just abrogated a major democratic reform and was a two-term incumbent in an increasingly anti-incumbent environment. What's more, his relationship to the wing of the Independence Party that controlled the mayoral nomination had gone south, perhaps irrevocably. The Bloomberg team found itself in the position of having to walk back from the self-inflicted rift.

The first approach to the Independence Party was made by Bloomberg pollster and adviser Doug Schoen, who had remained close to me, Newman, and the city party throughout the mayor's second term. Schoen asked me if we would take a call from the Bloomberg camp. With some attitude, I told him we would.

The first set of exploratory meetings involved Schoen, campaign manager Bradley Tusk, Fred Newman, Harry Kresky, and me at the townhouse in Greenwich Village where Newman and I lived. We'd known Tusk as an ally in 2003 during the campaign for nonpartisan elections. Tall and surprisingly fresh-faced, Tusk had a straightforward and nonabrasive style. Plus, he was smart. He knew he was walking into a political minefield.

The discussions were polite but strained. Tusk had taken the reins from Sheekey, and the message was that whatever bad blood had been created, whatever insult or insensitivities had been allowed, were all Sheekey's doings. Sheekey was now taking a backseat, and Tusk and Schoen were the top campaign people. Tusk was very direct. We can't win this without you, he said.

Newman was extremely candid. He used the term "bewildered" to describe his feelings about Bloomberg's walking away from the people who had supported him and his allying with someone bent on destroying them and the democratic fabric of the party. He said he wasn't angry. Much of the IP base was, though.

Tusk's job was to manage the fence mending by offering himself and a new regime that would respect the party and handle the partnership in good faith. Where Sheekey had been an elusive and unstable partner, Tusk would be available and present. As far as MacKay was concerned, Tusk didn't really know him and would have no contact with him. Moreover, he would do whatever he could to protect the city organization from any further incursions by MacKay. Newman asked whether Tusk had been authorized by Bloomberg to conduct the meetings and to ask for our support. Tusk said yes, he was representing the mayor's express directive. Newman told Tusk we were also meeting with the opposition.

Bloomberg was not the only fish in the sea, and—as in 2001—the Democratic Party believed it could play on Bloomberg's vulnerabilities, which were considerable, to finally win back City Hall with a black mayor. Bill Thompson, the city controller, was expected to be the Democratic Party nominee. He had a longstanding connection to Lenora Fulani, since both were active in education politics and were well-known figures in black political circles. He had been an outspoken opponent of nonpartisan elections.

In early 2009 Fulani set up a meeting with Thompson, his campaign manager Eduardo Castell, Newman, Kresky, and me to discuss Thompson's mayoral bid and the prospects for an IP endorsement. Thompson, a former president of the Board of Education and a progeny of the New York City black Democratic machine, was fired up about the term limits alteration and was ready to beat Bloomberg over the head with it. The discussion with

Thompson was cordial, and we asked several key questions. Could Thompson support nonpartisan elections? Could Thompson manage a retooling of the Democratic Party's hostile posture toward the IP?

Thompson's answer to the first question was decidedly "no," and to the second, equivocal at best. He would speak with other Democratic Party leaders about the matter. But he never managed to reach an effective detente. Our potential partnership with the Democrats was deflating rapidly.

On February 19, the *New York Times* reported on the meetings between the Bloomberg team and IP leaders, and word began to circulate that a rapprochement might be in the works.[28] Meanwhile, MacKay engineered a new set of allegations against members of the city IP organization. We told Tusk about the new charges, and he arranged to have intermediaries reach MacKay. Without further ado, the charges evaporated.

A face-to-face meeting with Bloomberg took place on March 17, St. Patrick's Day. The mayor arrived fresh from the parade, sporting a green sweater, in a chipper and friendly mood. He spent an hour at our townhouse (much more modest than his!), and we drew the contours of a deal. Bloomberg pledged to consider another pass at nonpartisan elections. He would put an initiative on the ballot that would allow the voters to reimpose a two-term limit. The IP would play a prominent role in the reelection campaign. Newman reminded Bloomberg that though we'd done this twice before, it was the first time we were doing it with Mike as a registered independent. We expected that to be a meaningful factor in what we could deliver on Election Day.

A few days later, Newman and I sat down again with *New York Times* reporter Michael Barbaro to fill him in on the meeting with the mayor and our decision to endorse him. Before the piece was published, I made a courtesy call to Castell to let the Thompson camp know that the Independence Party was going with Bloomberg and that the *Times* would run the story in the next few days. When I got off the phone with Castell, I told Newman that the 2009 mayoral race had just been decided.

At a meeting of the 90-member New York City IP executive committee, Newman made his case as to why a Bloomberg endorsement made sense. He told members—who were still angry with the mayor for his refusal to stand up to Frank MacKay's witch hunt against the city party—that despite his failures and shortcomings, Bloomberg was an independent, had governed New York City as an independent, and his approach to government had been good for the city. This was a moment, Newman argued, for independent leaders to stand up and say they would do what was best for New York, regardless of their personal complaints.

Then Bloomberg attended a meeting with the executive committee at the Vincci Avalon Hotel in midtown. It was packed to the rafters with press, who were invited to hear Bloomberg's opening remarks to the group. A closed-door discussion followed. When Bloomberg arrived, Stewart walked him through the room, introducing him to each member. The crowd was fully representative of the IP base—poor black women and men from the city's toughest neighborhoods, white Manhattan professionals, transit workers, social workers, and stockbrokers. The committee, by a vote of 95 percent, endorsed Bloomberg and awarded him the IP line. I called Tusk and the mayor to give them the news.

The campaign built heavily on the theme of Bloomberg's political independence: "Mayor Mike Bloomberg: Strong independent leadership to keep NYC working"; "Innovative solutions start with great ideas and independent leadership"; "His is the kind of visionary, nonpartisan leadership that puts politics aside and gets the job done"; "Progress, not politics." Bloomberg contributed $400,000 to the IPNYC and was careful with his giving to the state party so as not to inflame the passions around MacKay.[29] The message of political independence was everywhere, and Bloomberg pushed it aggressively. He even involved himself in the national organizing of IndependentVoting.org, as a special guest on my regular national conference call of the IndependentVoting.org networks, during which he spoke to 100 independent leaders about the challenges of governing as an independent.

Three days before the election, the IP held a citywide rally of 500 volunteers who would run neighborhood operations for "Bloomberg on C." It was a microcosm of independent New York. Multigenerational, multiracial, poor and well-heeled, all outspoken. The mayor, casually dressed and preternaturally relaxed, arrived with Diana Taylor to join the rally. Newman, by then in a wheelchair as his kidney disease had progressed significantly, introduced the mayor:

> I've been involved in independent politics since the very beginning. One thing that's happened on a national level—in Minnesota, in Connecticut, all over the country—is that many, many people who think that this is just a bunch of people who swing back and forth, say, "Well I can swing too, I'll use them, and then I'll abandon them." That's been the standard pattern, from Minnesota to Texas, to California . . . "I'll abandon them after I've gotten their votes, of course. Then I'll abandon them."
>
> Let me tell you the one person who hasn't done that. . . . That doesn't mean we agree on everything, it doesn't mean we always see it the same way. I think I'm in a position to say, and I hope you will trust me on this, Mike Bloomberg has never abandoned independent politics. If that isn't a sign of real political character I don't know what is. . . .
>
> And so I wanted to come here today for my blood, for my transfusion. . . . It's a very memorable day, an important day, and I wanted to be together with all of you . . . to support the real independent, the true independent, Mike Bloomberg. I wanted to also, for whatever it's worth, give my personal statement of support to this man, whom I feel very, very close to politically, because of what he stands for. He is indeed, a true independent. Thank you, Mike.

Bloomberg took the stage and crossed to where Newman was seated in his wheelchair to shake his hand. Then he went to the podium. "Fred," he said, "I'll never forget what you said. I hope I live up to the standards you have enunciated." The applause was thunderous.

It's difficult to describe what that moment was like. It seemed like a sudden tear in the fabric of the political universe, a momentary evaporation of all the vitriol and opportunism that soaks the New York political culture. Eight years of continuous public hammering on Newman and Fulani, eight years of sordid attempts by the city's media (especially the *Post*, the *Times*, and NY1), by the Democratic Party, and by top elected officials to sever Bloomberg's connection to the progressive wing of the independent movement, eight years of conflict within Bloomberg's inner circle and, surely, for Mike himself over the role the Independence Party had played in making his mayoralty—all were transformed in that one moment, and there was nothing but the hard-won political independence everyone in the room shared. For that moment, the partisan vultures couldn't do damage. For that moment, there was a speck of humanity in the political game.

Of course, as soon as Bloomberg exited the rally, the reporters and TV cameras descended on him. He refused to talk to them. I did. And when they started throwing baiting questions at me, I told them they were out of line and out of date. I wasn't in any mood to handle them. I just wanted them to shut up for once.

On Election Day, 48 hours after the rally, Mike Bloomberg was reelected mayor by a margin of 55,000 votes. The Democrats had, once again, failed to win over a majority of New York City voters. But this win was different. The Independence Party polled 150,000 votes on its Column C line—nearly 30 percent of Bloomberg's total vote, double the IP vote in 2005, and the highest independent vote in a New York City mayoral race since 1949.

Unsurprisingly, the Independence Party vote total was barely reported in the press. But the size and scale of the independent vote was a major marker. Independents everywhere saw it as a sign that the movement was maturing. And, it gave Bloomberg the popular mandate he needed to proceed with another try at nonpartisan elections. Bloomberg appointed a new Charter Revision Commission in 2010, making good on his promise to give the voters the chance to reset the term limits law and to explore nonpartisan elections.

Several other changes had occurred since 2003, in addition to the IP's 150,000 votes. After discussions with Fulani, Newman, and his own attorney, Michael Hardy, Al Sharpton went on record saying that he was open to supporting nonpartisans. Howard Wolfson, formerly the Democratic Party strategist and chief warrior against nonpartisan elections in 2003, was now working for Bloomberg at City Hall as his communications director. And the city's oldest and most prestigious good-government group—the Citizens Union— was under new leadership and had changed its 2003 position opposing nonpartisan elections. In June 2010 the Citizens Union issued a 40-page report that favored the adoption of the nonpartisan reform. Under the stewardship of its new executive director, Dick Dadey, and its prime advocate for the change, John Avlon, the report stated, "Increasing voter eligibility is essential in a city that is effectively electing officials in closed partisan primaries where the proportion of registered voters is as low as five percent. Our remedy is this reform [top-two open primaries]—we can increase voter participation and politicians' accountability by opening up New York City's election process."[30]

But as in 2002 and 2003, Democratic Party opposition to the reform was fierce. The Citizens Union's change of heart did not sway other good-government groups. Opposition among the unions and elected officials remained strong, and, most crushing to Bloomberg, the *New York Times* reiterated its opposition in an April editorial.[31] Then, in August, Sharpton, who for months had taken a wait-and-see posture, came out decisively *against* nonpartisan elections. Three days later, Bloomberg announced that he would recommend to his Charter Revision Commission that they *not put* the nonpartisan election question on the ballot.

The day before he went public, Mike called to tell me what he was going to do. He said the coalition he needed to get the reform over the top simply wasn't there. I disagreed. I told him that he and the independent movement together had become more powerful than the *New York Times* and the Democratic machine. He was unconvinced. He told me he still believed that the greatest legacy he could leave the city would be nonpartisan elections. Unfortunately, he said, it wasn't in the cards. In August the commission voted to place a referendum on the ballot to restore two-term limits. It passed in November with 73.9 percent of the vote.[32]

As for Bloomberg's dilemma, it was never resolved. Caught in the constant crossfire between a progressive independent movement that wanted structural political change and new coalitions, and the anti-reform Democrats who wanted neither, he couldn't win over or neutralize the insiders. But he did help the outsiders grow. That growth has been invested several times over in a struggling but energized up-from-the-bottom independent movement.

EIGHT

THE PARTIES VS. THE PEOPLE

MICHAEL LEWIS IS AN IMPOSING MAN. SIX-FOOT-SIX, 340 POUNDS, BARREL-CHESTED, he looks like someone who could crush an opponent without even a sideways glance. Lewis played semipro football in his younger days. Today he is married, with two young daughters, and has worked as a prelitigation specialist in the financial credit industry. It's a business that Lewis feels uncomfortable about. "It's hard to make a living off of other people's misfortune," he says in a gentle voice that seems at odds with his physical stature. He would like to change careers. But the economy being what it is, it's hard to make that change, especially in a place like Kentucky, where jobs are scarce and wages are low.

Michael Lewis is an independent. When you talk with him, you realize that it's as much an attitude, a posture, a sensibility, as it is a political position. He doesn't like political parties; he feels they have too much control. He wants independent voters to have more political power. Kentucky is a "closed primary" state—meaning candidates are nominated through primary elections in which only party members can vote, not independents. Lewis took up the cause of open primaries in 2008, after he met a group of local activists working with IndependentVoting.org to introduce a bill into the Kentucky legislature to allow independents to vote in primary contests. The bill was defeated in committee, but its sponsor, Representative Jimmy Higdon of Lebanon, a Republican, took notice of the voice independent voters were gaining in the state. When a special election was called for an open state senate seat in the 14th District, Higdon decided to make a run and reached out to Lewis for his help in delivering a campaign message to the district's 3,500 independent voters. Lewis agreed, on the condition that Higdon would introduce the open primaries bill in the next legislative session. Higdon pledged that he would. Lewis mailed personal letters to several thousand nonaligned voters, promoting Higdon's support for open primaries that would end the independents' exclusion from first-round voting. Higdon won the special election and credits the support from independents with putting him over the top.

At the GOP victory party, where Republican luminaries and good ol' boys hung out at the bar, Lewis was the man of the hour. A friend asked him afterward whether he was recognized at the event. "I'm kinda hard to miss," he said. But it wasn't his size that got him noticed. It was that Lewis, a grassroots independent, had stirred up a base around a political reform issue. They'd sent Higdon to the state senate on that basis.

Local Republicans were busy slapping Lewis on the back, buying him beers, and inviting him to join the GOP. "Why don't you come with us?" they asked. "No thanks," said Lewis. "We've got other things to focus on right now."

And he did. He founded Independent Kentucky together with Alexander Kemble and several of their friends. They affiliated with IndependentVoting.org, and Lewis soon called Higdon, asking him to deliver on his campaign promise. Higdon introduced the bill on January 6, 2010, and Lewis traveled to Frankfort in February to walk the halls of the state capitol and drum up support.

Along the way, he ran into Senator Julian Carroll, a Democrat and former governor of the Bluegrass State. Lewis pressed him about the open primary bill, about making sure that everyone in Kentucky, regardless of their party affiliation, would be admitted to every round of voting. Carroll, now 80 years old and once part of a circle of upstart Democratic legislators called the Young Turks, was incensed beyond reason by Lewis's appeal. "Well, if you don't like it, then move to another country," he told Lewis in the capitol hallway. A CNN crew following Lewis's campaign captured the encounter on video. Lewis was astonished. With the help of IndependentVoting.org's national organizer Gwen Mandell, the exchange went viral.

That day the Republican-controlled state senate, at Higdon's urging, passed Lewis's open primary bill. It was defeated, however, in the Democrat-controlled house. CNN's David Mattingly pressed Senator Carroll about the issue on camera while the voting was underway. "If they want a party," said Carroll, "fine, we'll create them a party, and then they can have their own party that believes in their own principles." Mattingly wasn't satisfied. He told Carroll: "Independents don't want to have their own party. They want to vote for Republicans or Democrats." Carroll was unperturbed. "I don't care what they want. I'm telling you how we operate a democracy in America. We operate a democracy in America with the two-party system."[1]

Lewis's battle is far from over. In 2011 Higdon again introduced an open primary bill. This time it failed to pass by one vote. Lewis understands that reforming the process and building a movement take time. "We continue to gain momentum," he says. "The independent voters of Kentucky are gaining ground." Lewis is, in effect, fighting two causes. One is challenging the Kentucky closed primary system—in place in numerous other states, too—that permits parties to exclude voters from the nominating process.[2] The other cause is to organize independent voters to become a force for changing the political structure without having to form a third party. Unfortunately, Carroll's notion that if independents want to be recognized, they need a party of their own is conventional wisdom in the political establishment. For Carroll, that no doubt translates into *Get them out of the way and over to the sidelines.*

But for Lewis, and now for many hundreds of grassroots independent activists leading state and local challenges to the hard-wired partisanship of the system, the goal isn't to create a new party. It's about making the *process itself* a cause; it's about new forms of political expression that allow independents and all Americans to move the country away from partisan politics.

There is no real third-party movement in America today, in spite of the recent *ABC News/Washington Post* poll showing that 61 percent of Americans would like to see an independent alternative to the Democrats and Republicans in the upcoming presidential election. But there is an *anti-party* movement, one that is being organized and shaped by diverse influences. The emerging conflict over closed primaries, open primaries, and nonparty primaries, in which the rights of the people are pitted against the rights of the parties, embodies a uniquely twenty-first-century question. Are political parties the vehicles through which the American people want to self-organize and self-govern?

Today, 84 percent of Americans have an unfavorable view of Congress.[3] This Congress? Surely. Any Congress? Maybe. Which raises another question. Given the partisan nature of the system, is it possible for Congress to behave differently? Many feel it's impossible without structural changes to the party system itself. Mickey Edwards, who served in Congress for 18 years from Oklahoma, put it this way when he proposed a set of structural reforms to the electoral and congressional process: "The problem is not division but partisanship—advantage-seeking by private clubs whose central goal is to win political power."[4]

The political parties are the vehicles to which Americans turn to exercise their political will. But that exercise seems increasingly futile. A clear majority of Americans, for example, believe (and experience!) that income disparity is getting wider, but they have no power to do anything about it. The Occupy Wall Street events of 2011 are a reaction to that, and so are the polls showing many Americans sympathetic to those protests. No matter who is elected, the special interests, the elite, and the insiders still run the show.

Thus, reform of the process is becoming strategically important and popular among the American people. Michael Lewis's battles in Kentucky are no mere local affair. They signify activities of an emerging anti-party movement with a new social and political fabric. And there is no better place to pick up its thread than inside the jacket pocket of a California state senator, Abel Maldonado.

It was February 2009. The California state legislature was under lockdown in Sacramento. Governor Arnold Schwarzenegger, a Republican, and Assembly majority leader Karen Bass, a Democrat, had reached an agreement on the long-stalled state budget. But legislative leaders couldn't cobble together the two-thirds majority required to pass it. Late into the night of February 18, entreaties and offers were made to the holdouts. The $143 billion budget deal hung in the balance.

Somewhere along the line, a call was made to Abel Maldonado. A first-generation Mexican American, whose family had prospered in the fertile farmlands of the coastal region, Maldonado was considered a moderate Republican. Schwarzenegger, who would later tap him to serve as lieutenant governor, once described Maldonado as being "into bipartisanship and postpartisanship," someone who "makes decisions based on what's best for the people rather than what's best for the party."[5] Maldonado listened to the arguments for passing the budget, which included tax increases he had previously foresworn. That's when he reached into his jacket pocket and pulled out a piece of paper that, Maldonado says, he had been carrying around for 14 years. On the paper was the wording for a top-two open primary initiative that would restyle the whole of California's partisan primary system. Maldonado would vote for the budget, including the tax increases, but he wanted something else added to the package: The legislature must place before the voters a ballot initiative that would abolish party primaries and establish public primaries instead, in which all voters of all parties or of no party would be permitted to vote. The top two vote-getters would go on to compete in a general election, hence the name Top Two.

At first the legislative leadership balked. Maldonado says he put the paper back in his pocket and walked out of the negotiations, telling them there would be no deal. But sometime in the middle of the night, he says, he got a call. He put his jacket back on, checked to make sure the paper was still folded inside his pocket, and returned. Bass and company were ready to agree. Maldonado became one of six Republicans to vote for the budget. The legislature, until that moment hamstrung by an immutable partisan divide, authorized a ballot initiative for June 2010, proposing a shift to Top Two nonpartisan elections.

Jason Olson, an organizer of California's IndependentVoice. Org,[6] read the news of the Maldonado trade with interest. In his early thirties, Olson had been an independent since he first became a voter. His grandfather signed on to be a union organizer in 1929, and Olson says he has activist politics in his blood. He worked to pass a campaign finance reform initiative in California in 1996 that fell short. Later, he played competitive poker, and in 2000 he caught C-SPAN coverage of Lenora Fulani speaking to college students about the Reform Party's left/center/right coalition. He was captivated by the idea of the alliance, called the 800 number for more information, and soon became a part of the IndependentVoting.org team. When the budget deal was reported, he called the national headquarters to update us and then placed a call to Maldonado.

Open primaries already had a turbulent history in California. In 1996, Prop 198 passed with 60 percent of the vote, changing California's closed primary to a "blanket primary." In a blanket primary, each voter's ballot lists every candidate regardless of party affiliation and allows the voter to choose freely among them. For example, a voter could cast a ballot in a Democratic primary for governor, a Republican primary for U.S. senator, and a Libertarian primary for congress, mixing and matching as she or he sees fit.

When the blanket primary went into effect in 1998, the state saw an increase in voter participation of 7.5 percent or 1.2 million voters. However, the admittance of the state's nearly two million nonaligned voters and the uptick in voter participation were not well received by the political parties. California's Democratic and Republican parties, joined by the Libertarian Party and the Peace and Freedom Party, filed suit in federal court against the initiative as soon as it passed. They claimed that the blanket primary violated a political party's First Amendment right of association in that the party's nominees could be determined by voters who, at best, had refused to affiliate with the party and, at worst, were hostile to the principles of the party.

The case, *California Democratic Party v. Jones*,[7] turned out to be a landmark, and as time went on, the *Jones* decision became a stark, legal impediment to open primary reform. At the start of the litigation, the federal district court described Prop 198 as "the latest development in a history of political reform measures that began in the Progressive Era."[8] It upheld the blanket primary reform, stating that the new system "enhances the democratic nature of the election process and the representativeness of elected officials."[9] The Ninth Circuit Court of Appeals affirmed the district court ruling.[10] But the Supreme Court took a different view.

Jones came before the U.S. Supreme Court in 2000, a remarkable year for Supreme Court rulings on electoral matters (*Bush v. Gore* was also rendered then). The court reversed the lower court decisions by a vote of seven to two. The majority opinion, authored by Judge Antonin Scalia, endorsed the role political parties play in America's electoral process.

Calling representative democracy "unimaginable" without citizens having the ability "to band together in promoting among the electorate candidates who espouse their political views," Scalia asserted that "the formation of national political parties was almost concurrent with the formation of the Republic itself." Concluding that a party's right to freedom of association was protected under the First Amendment, and that "a corollary of the right to associate is the right not to associate," Scalia held that there was no compelling state interest to prevent parties from limiting the universe of primary voters.[11]

In his dissent in *Jones,* Justice John Paul Stevens argued that "the so-called 'right not to associate'" was misapplied by Scalia. "A political party, like any other association, may refuse to allow nonmembers to participate in the party's decisions when it is conducting its own affairs," Stevens wrote. "But an election, unlike a convention or caucus, is a public affair."[12]

The *Jones* decision invalidated Washington State's blanket primary as well, but open primary advocates developed a well-crafted end-run around Scalia's objections: the Top Two model. If party primaries could invoke an impenetrable First Amendment claim, then a new kind of primary would be needed, one that was indisputably, as Justice Stevens had suggested, "a public affair."

Initiative 872 was put on the Washington State ballot in 2004. A citizen's initiative for Top Two, this new version abolished party primaries altogether and substituted a two-step public primary in its place, thus avoiding the constitutional pitfalls enshrined in *Jones*. It passed with 60 percent support,[13] and its constitutionality was upheld by the U.S. Supreme Court.[14] However, a similar attempt in California in 2004 (IndependentVoice.Org was part of this coalition) met with blistering resistance from the parties and was defeated by the voters, garnering only 46 percent support.[15]

So, for Olson and the independent leaders in his circle, the prospect of another shot at a Top Two primary system for California was enticing. The political climate had changed since 2004. By 2010, California had 3.5 million nonaligned voters[16] (the number of independents had risen by 84 percent since 1998), and they were banging on the door of party control. Voters had already passed an unusually potent independent redistricting plan in 2008 and were hungry for more nonpartisan reforms. As Olson reached out to Maldonado in an effort to join forces in the campaign for Prop 14, Schwarzenegger endorsed the initiative, as did the American Association of Retired Persons (AARP), the Chamber of Commerce, and the California Independent Voter Network (CAIVN). CNN ran a four-minute segment on the California battle as part of its *Broken Government* series featuring Olson and discussing the potential impact the system would have on independent voters statewide.

Soon Maldonado and Olson were hitting the campaign trail together. Maldonado, the renegade legislator, and Olson, the independent organizer, took their message to the editorial board of the

San Francisco Chronicle on April 1. Maldonado pitched Prop 14 as the antidote to broken government in Sacramento. Olson argued that the rise of independents in California and across the country was itself a movement against partisanship. The inclusion of independents would open the door to changes in the political culture. The *Chronicle's* editorial, published on April 25, enthusiastically endorsed Prop 14: "Californians who decline to state a party preference are the fastest growing group on the state's voter rolls. They now account for one out of five voters. Yet California's system for electing candidates to state and federal offices remains locked in an era when party politics reigned."[17]

As major newspapers followed the *Chronicle's* lead by recommending the passage of Prop 14, the minor parties, particularly the Libertarians and Greens, dug in against it. Minor parties have historically been champions of opening the political process, fighting against unfair ballot access restrictions, the exclusion of independent candidates from debates, and the second-class status afforded independent campaigns generally. But the prospect of a Top Two primary raised special problems for minor party leaders. Could they put aside their investment in a guaranteed spot on the general election ballot to support a measure that opened up the process for unaffiliated voters and limited the power of the major parties?

For California's minor parties, appearing on the general election ballot is the Holy Grail even though they poll only 2 to 3 percent in most local elections. In fact, the vast majority of third-party candidates elected to office in that state won their seats in municipal and county races already run in the nonpartisan Top Two format. Nonetheless, all six ballot-qualified parties— Democrat, Republican, Green, Libertarian, Peace & Freedom, American Independent—held a joint press conference on May 11 in Sacramento to announce their shared opposition to Proposition 14. The Democrats and Republicans were exultant. Having the third-party club opposed to Prop 14 meant the Big Two could claim that independents opposed the reform. Leading Libertarian Richard Winger, editor of *Ballot Access News* and a respected advocate for independent and minor party candidates, spent long hours advancing arguments against Top Two and accusing its supporters of being anti-independent.

The highest-profile encounter between the independent voters and the minor parties featured Ralph Nader and Harry Kresky. It was ironic that the two were on opposite sides since both are crusaders for democracy reform. Kresky had been a key member of Nader's legal team in 2004 when the Democratic National Committee conspired to remove Nader from as many presidential ballots as possible, forcing Nader to litigate his way onto the ballot in numerous states. On that score, the two were in complete agreement. But Nader opposed Prop 14, calling Top Two "an incumbency protection plan that restricts choice and could eliminate minor parties." If not defeated, he said, Prop 14 "will risk further entrenching the two-party system."[18]

Kresky, initially surprised at the stringent party bias inherent in Nader's view, called Prop 14 "an important step towards nonpartisan governance" and pointed out ways for minor parties to *increase* their impact under the Top Two system: "Voters will be voting for candidates, not parties, and there is a real opportunity for coalitions of independents, parties (minor and major), and party members to join together to support reform-oriented candidates. Under Proposition 14, an effective coalition can propel a candidate not favored by the party establishment (major and minor) to round two, with a real chance to win."[19]

But what most upset Kresky about Nader's rejection of Top Two was the fact that it placed Nader squarely in the camp of the two major parties. "Since Proposition 14 is an attempt to loosen the hold that the major parties have on our democracy by their iron-fisted control of the nominating process," Kresky argued, "it is no surprise that the major parties—whose tyranny Nader denounces—are doing everything they can to defeat it."[20]

Even with the Big Two and the third party coalition campaigning actively against it, and even though the legislature had put the initiative on the ballot on primary day when party loyalists—not independents—are used to voting, Prop 14 passed with 54 percent of the vote, the highest margin for a political reform initiative in California in more than a dozen years. Now it was the independents' turn to be exultant. The *New York Times*, in a front-page article headlined "California Voting Change Could Signal Big Political Shift," reported that Californians "voted Tuesday to radically rejigger elections in the nation's most populous state."[21] Maldonado, Schwarzenegger, IndependentVoice.Org, the AARP,

and the Chamber of Commerce celebrated the win at press conferences in Los Angeles and in Sacramento. "The voters made a clear
and decisive statement that the way to fix broken government is to
expand democracy, contain the control exercised by political parties, and give greater power to the people," IndependentVoice.Org's
Joyce Dattner concluded.[22] Schwarzenegger said, "Coupled with
redistricting, Proposition 14 will change the political landscape in
California—finally giving voters the power to truly hold politicians
accountable."[23] And Maldonado told Dylan Ratigan after the victory that the passage of Prop 14 was historic.[24] "It allows 'decline to
states' and independents to have a voice," he said.[25]

If the state legislatures are one forum where nonpartisan reform is being pushed onto the agenda, and popular initiatives
(where voters have that right) are another, the courts are becoming yet a third battleground where the conflict between the parties and the people plays out. Beginning in 2007, in a prelude to
the Tea Party movement's reassertion of social conservatism inside
the GOP, self-described conservative Republican networks in open
primary states began to press for closing their primaries. For these
networks, the influence of independent voters represented a threat
to their core ideological beliefs and, apparently, to their competitive position in local GOP politics. The first state to experience this
backlash was Idaho.

In 2007 Mitch Campbell formed the American Independent
Movement (AIM) of Idaho, a grassroots organization representing Idaho's 750,000 independent voters. Campbell, an investment

consultant from Twin Falls, found IndependentVoting.org online and was attracted to its progressive outlook. In February 2007 he testified against H185, a Republican-sponsored bill that sought to end Idaho's system of open primary elections, in place for 37 years. Though dominated by a Republican majority, the legislature defeated the proposed measure.

But when Mitch Campbell called IndependentVoting.org's national headquarters in the spring of 2008, he was deeply alarmed. The Republican Party had decided to bypass the legislature it controlled and file a lawsuit seeking to have Idaho's open primary system declared unconstitutional.

At their state convention in January 2008, the conservative wing pressured the party's central committee to adopt a closed primary rule, which contained a "trigger" stating that if the legislature did not act in favor of closed primaries, the party would automatically file suit. Leading the closed primary caucus was a former state assemblyman named Rod Beck.

"From my experience, Beck and other closed primary advocates represent the fringes," Campbell explains. "If Beck and others of like mind can prevent independents from voting in primaries, they can more easily select and elect extremist candidates who can control the parties and the government. That's why they want to close the primaries." Confident in the Supreme Court's *California Democratic Party v. Jones* decision of 2000 and antagonized by the success of the party's moderate wing, Beck began to move the Idaho lawsuit along.

While Republican Ben Ysursa, as Idaho's secretary of state, would defend the open primary system in court—Ysursa was not a fan of Beck's initiative and thought it unnecessary since the GOP already held every statewide office—he would not necessarily represent the specific interests of independents. Yet, according to Boise State University's latest survey, independents were 37 percent of Idaho voters, and they had no direct representation in the proceeding.[26] Campbell, AIM, and IndependentVoting.org believed independents needed their own voice in the case, since they would be immediately and adversely affected by a shift to a partisan system. On July 1, 2008, eleven independent voters together with AIM and Committee for a Unified Independent Party (CUIP) filed court papers asking the federal judge to admit them as defendant-intervenors in the case. Boise attorney Gary Allen, a veteran of the Perot movement and the Reform Party who had become a prominent Idaho Democrat, joined the legal team headed by Harry Kresky. At a hearing ordered by Judge B. Lynn Winmill, Republican Party attorney Eric Sutton opposed the intervention, claiming that the case was only a dispute between the Republican Party and the state government, that it did not concern the electorate, and that the rights of independent voters would be represented by the secretary of state.

But Judge Winmill was not convinced. On August 19 he granted defendant-intervenor status to the applicants, stating it would be "putting the cart before the horse to prejudge the intervenors' right" when voting rights are at stake. Winmill's decision was the first time that independent voters and organizations representing them won the right to directly participate in a legal controversy between a political party and a state government.[27]

The court battle raged for two more years. In late 2010 Judge Winmill, well aware that the case before him was a political hot potato, insisted that the Republican Party produce evidence of the injury that the open primary system caused and ordered that a trial be held.

In addition to the legal arguments raised on both sides, Kresky and Allen asked the judge to consider the wider political dimensions of the case. They pointed out that the Republican Party was seeking greater control over the electoral framework at a time when the number of political independents—and dissatisfaction with partisanship in our elections and government—was on the rise. For independents, the Republican assertion that the First Amendment guaranteed their right to control the electoral system was more than just an affront to political choice; it muzzled their desire to reshape American elections and government.

Five months after the trial, in March 2011 Judge B. Lynn Winmill issued a ruling in favor of the GOP. Winmill relied heavily on the *Jones* decision: "Like the blanket primary system in *Jones*, Idaho's current open primary system, as applied, forces the Idaho Republican Party to associate with, and have their nominees and positions determined by, those who have refused to affiliate with the party."[28]

In the wake of the decision, the Idaho legislature moved quickly to institute a new closed primary system based on a partisan registration process. The legislature also passed a measure to reimburse the Republican Party $100,000 for their legal costs. Governor Butch Otter signed the bill. While Otter opposed closed primaries, he said the court's decision had given him no choice.[29]

Even before the Idaho trial was concluded, word traveled through Republican circles that any state party wishing for greater control over its nominating process might consider a similar strategy. Another solidly red state, South Carolina, would be next up, and this time the political dynamics and the results would be different.

It began as it had in Idaho, when Wayne Griffin, chairman of the South Carolina Independence Party, got wind of a plan by some Republicans to ask the federal court to close the state's primaries.

Griffin and his brother are part of a community of black small businessmen in Greer. They run an insurance business and are active in their church. Always an independent thinker who delighted in upsetting the political apple cart, Griffin had supported Lenora Fulani's independent presidential campaign in 1988. He still loves telling the story of how Fulani's southern regional coordinator, Bob Friedman, knocked on his door one day. "What's this white guy doing at my door?" he asked his wife. "This can't be good." But it turned out Friedman was collecting signatures to put a black female independent on the ballot in South Carolina. Griffin signed, and he and Friedman soon became friends.

With Fulani and Friedman, he jumped into the Perot movement after the 1992 campaign and went on to lead the Independence

Party of South Carolina (for a time it was the Reform Party affiliate in South Carolina). In 1999 he was elected to the Greer city council. In early 2008, he ran a successful "Independents for Obama" campaign on black radio stations with the message, "The Democratic Party establishment—now run by Bill and Hillary Clinton—sees the country in terms of old labels, old coalitions, and old tactics. They think change comes from the top. But the change I am part of is coming from the bottom." Obama's breakthrough victory in the South Carolina Democratic primary was propelled by the very coalition of black and independent voters that Griffin had energized.

In early June 2010 Griffin called CUIP's national headquarters in New York. He had seen an article in the *Greenville News* about a Republican Party lawsuit that aimed to close the primaries. "Seems like shades of Idaho to me," he told Nancy Ross, co-director of national organizing. "We've had the open primary here for almost 50 years, but I guess the Republicans want to shut it down. Can we do something?"

South Carolina differed from Idaho in one important respect. The state has a large black community, and a key question was whether changing to a closed primary system would negatively impact the black community as a whole.

Griffin began to reach out to members of the South Carolina legislative black caucus, all Democrats, to alert them to the situation and to discuss its implications. Meanwhile, Michelle McCleary, a longtime IndependentVoting.org activist based in New York, followed up on Griffin's outreach, connecting with

Representative Joe Neal, a progressive Democrat who has been in the legislature since 1993.

Neal was immediately sympathetic to the cause. Open primaries had been enacted in South Carolina as part of the repeal of Jim Crow laws. Neal feared that reverting to closed primaries would open the door to political resegregation, with white voters joining the Republican Party in order to have a voice in the dominant party, leaving African Americans isolated in a marginalized Democratic Party. Neal agreed to join the suit and organize other members of his caucus to do the same.

On February 4, 2011, Kresky and local counsel Fletcher Smith filed a motion to intervene in the federal district court on behalf of 13 members of the legislative black caucus, three South Carolina independent voters, the South Carolina Independence Party, the South Carolina Constitution Party, the Progressive Network Education Fund, the Columbia Tea Party (which had broken from the state Tea Party organization, which it considered too tethered to the Republican Party), and IndependentVoting.org. The case was followed with considerable interest, both by national and state Republican figures who preferred to maintain open primaries but were afraid to publicly challenge their own party's right wing, and by black leaders sympathetic to Griffin's and Neal's concerns. One of them, Al Sharpton, hosted Neal, Griffin, Smith, and me on his daily radio show, *The Al Sharpton Show*.

Unlike the Idaho case, which languished in federal court for nearly three years, this one moved forward quickly. Three months after the filing, Judge Michelle Childs granted the coalition inter-venor status. Three weeks later, she granted the state's request for summary judgment and rejected the Republican Party's claim that the state's open primary was unconstitutional.

Judge Childs hung her decision on an unusual feature of the South Carolina election code. Unlike Idaho, South Carolina law gives parties an "opt out." If 75 percent of the delegates at a state convention vote to opt out of a primary and choose a candidate themselves, they are permitted to do so. This gave the judge the circumstances she needed to avoid the conclusions of *California Democratic Party v. Jones*. Because South Carolina law provided multiple avenues by which a party could nominate candidates, Judge Childs ruled that "South Carolina's open primary laws do not facially burden political parties' right to freedom of associa-tion."[30] As expected, the Republican Party then asked the court to grant a trial, to which Judge Childs agreed.

In the meantime, independents in other states were and are pressing the cause. Ted Downing, an outspoken former Arizona Democratic state legislator turned independent, is spearheading an effort to put a Top Two initiative on the ballot in 2012. Downing says, "I can tell you as a person who was elected, the thing that can-didates and politicians fear the most is not an argument. They fear an election."[31] Arizona, dominated by conservative Republicans, has been the focus of intense political fights over immigration and redistricting. But it also has had significant growth in the number of independent voters—the percentage of registered independents in Arizona rose from 27.6 percent in 2008 to 32.8 percent in 2011. Polls show 71 percent of Arizona independents favoring a shift to Top Two. Downing and Larry Sakin, a prominent progressive reformer, have helped to shape a Top Two coalition that includes the former Democratic mayor of Phoenix, Paul Johnson, who recently became an independent, Republican Bill Konopnicki, who served in the Arizona House of Representatives, and Janelle Wood, who ran for governor as an independent in 2010, among others. Downing and Sakin drafted the initiative to prevent the legislature from favoring any political parties in the process of its implementation. Unlike California, no statewide elected officials have endorsed the initiative, making the Arizona reform campaign much more of an up-from-the-bottom effort.

These nonpartisan reform battles are early political flashpoints for a movement in which the *process* itself is becoming the core political concern. The constitutional controversies arise as independents themselves are rising.

In his latest blockbuster, *The Origins of Political Order*, Francis Fukuyama gives the problem a universal gloss. "The story of how political institutions developed cannot be told without understanding the complementary process of political decay. Human institutions are 'sticky;' that is, they persist over time and are changed only with great difficulty. Institutions that are created to meet one set of conditions often survive even when those conditions change or disappear, and the failure to adapt appropriately entails political decay."[32] A democratic political system that is both "sticky" and self-perpetuating is extremely difficult to reform or to dislodge. America's major political parties are among the "stickiest" of institutions. As Scalia noted, they arose immediately after the birth of the Republic. While not mentioned in the Constitution, they have survived civil war, westward expansion, industrialization, women's suffrage, prohibition, numerous reform movements, mass labor unrest, and two world wars. Yet, they now face resistance to their hold on the electoral and governing process. Millions of Americans see them as the major impediment to effective governance, and to fair and open democracy. Predictably, the parties become more partisan and more authoritarian in response.

Open and public primaries are not a complete solution to the political crisis by any means. But it's absolutely essential to work toward changing the process in ways that create opportunities for new things to happen. As simple as that sounds, the resistance to it is profound. Just ask Michael Lewis or Michael Bloomberg.

At this point, the political power of independents rests in being outsiders, in not being attached to any party, major or minor. This movement-in-the-making changes the political environment by changing the rules of the game. And, the collective activity of working together to change the rules develops the movement. Could a new *kind* of party emerge in that changed and changing environment? It could. But for it to represent an actual power shift, it will need to have roots in the independent movement that is evolving and a connection to its leaders, its infrastructure, and its issues.

NINE

BLACK AMERICA AND INDEPENDENT POLITICS

May God write us down as asses if ever again we are found putting our trust in either the Republican or the Democratic Parties.[1]

—W.E.B. Du Bois

IN MARCH 1972, EIGHT THOUSAND BLACK ACTIVISTS MET IN GARY, INDIANA, AT THE first National Black Political Convention. The turbulence of the 1960s, the passage of the Civil Rights and Voting Rights Acts, the assassinations of Malcolm X, Fred Hampton, and Dr. Martin Luther King Jr., and the intractability of poverty and social despair brought together a diverse cross-section of black America to shape a political strategy.

In the Gary Declaration, the convention called for a "new Black Politics." Under the heading "The Politics of Social Transformation," the declaration summarized the convention's purpose:

So we come to Gary confronted with a choice. But it is not the old convention question of which candidate shall we support, the pointless question of who is to preside over a decaying and unsalvageable system. No, if we come to Gary out of the realities of the Black communities of this land, then the only real choice for us is whether or not we will live by the truth we know, whether we will move to organize independently, move to struggle for fundamental transformation, for the creation of new directions, towards a concern for the life and the meaning of Man. Social transformation or social destruction, those are our only real choices.[2]

The Gary Convention was a microcosm of competing currents in black politics, including divisions over the tactical question of how to shape the black community's participation in electoral politics. Thirty years before the opportunity arose for African Americans to partner with white independents in a black and independent antipartisan alliance, the Gary Convention debated the question of how to shape a strategy for black empowerment. Should it be based in the Democratic Party or through an independent party? Historian Ron Walters summed up that core conflict in *Black Presidential Politics in America*.

The second major issue was the creation of a Black political party. Although strong sentiment had been voiced for such a step before the convention by persons such as Jesse Jackson, when the discussion came to the floor, Jackson and the leader of the Ohio delegation, Ron Daniels, strongly counseled delegates that a convention proclamation alone would not result in the formation of such a party. Rather, they suggested that if the grassroots work was accomplished which was considered to be a prerequisite to the formation of such a party, the party would naturally evolve. This evasive tactic prevailed, and the focus shifted to the details necessary to construct a continuing organizational mechanism for grassroots mobilization which would come to be known as the National Black Political Assembly.[3]

The dilemma faced by those assembled in Gary was not new to the black community. African Americans could not by themselves win equality, justice, or empowerment. As a large voting bloc but still a minority, African Americans needed to coalesce with partners. Yet, in doing so in the past they had seen their interests subordinated to the dominant power players in the political parties and movements they joined.[4]

Lenora Fulani assessed the dilemma faced by the Gary debate in an article for the journal *Souls:*

... a national Black political convention was held in Gary, Indiana at which the question of whether the Democratic Party could be made to serve as a vehicle for Black empowerment was hotly debated. In the end, the convention settled on the strategy of electing Blacks, as Democrats, to public office rather than creating an independent third party. But in a ringing keynote address, the mayor of Gary, Richard Hatcher—the first African American elected to govern a major city—warned that this would be the "last chance" for the Democratic Party; if the strategy failed, Black people would "cross the Rubicon" by forming an independent party based in communities of color and welcoming progressive whites.[5]

The black independent party envisioned, or evaded—as Walters suggests—never materialized. But the almost inexorable drift toward race-based strategies via the Democratic Party did. At the time of the Gary Convention, it is estimated that there were 2,264 black elected officials in America. Twenty-five years later, the number was 8,936, an increase of 294 percent. But even as the black community achieved larger and more visible levels of political representation, it was increasingly tethered to the Democrats.

Expanding the roster of black elected officials was propelled by the push for single-member districts, where dominantly black (or Latino, or Asian) legislative districts could be carved to ensure a particular outcome.[6] While this boosted the numbers of black representatives, it also cemented the power position of the dominant party, which, in the case of majority black districts, meant cementing the power of the Democratic Party. After all, it was the Democratic Party that brokered the creation of the black majority districts in the various state legislatures. Once those districts had been established, an incumbent could only be challenged in a party primary, since the Democratic nominee would invariably win the general election. President Lyndon Johnson's passage of the Civil

Rights and Voting Rights Acts combined with the devastating loss of more radical and independent black leaders had rooted black voters en masse in the Democratic Party. Thus, the Gary strategy yielded an unbreakable partisan bond. Empowerment, in this instance, meant immobility. And immobility meant black voters would be taken for granted. The new politic for black America so vividly imagined in the Gary Declaration never happened. Black people were Democrats, plain and simple.

Ironically, it was Jesse Jackson—arguably a founding father of the Gary Convention's Democratic Party tactic—who set out to respond to its consequences with his two insurgent presidential campaigns in 1984 and 1988.

For all of his grassroots popularity, Jackson was still sidelined by the party hierarchs. When Lenora Fulani made her first independent presidential run in 1988, a campaign she called "Two Roads Are Better Than One," she supported Jackson's primary bid. (Jackson's Democratic Party bid was the first road; Fulani's independent run was the second.) But the party accepted his nearly seven million primary votes with barely a nod, refused to consider him for the vice presidential slot with nominee Michael Dukakis, and neglected to inform Jackson of the choice of Senator Lloyd Bentsen. Jackson learned of the vice presidential choice from a reporter as he arrived at the airport in Washington, DC. Standing outside of the Democratic Convention in Atlanta that summer, as Jackson was dismissed by his own party, Fulani told 3,000 supporters that Jackson was a great leader but had led them to the wrong place. Fulani went on to poll a quarter of a million votes and establish a new beachhead for independent politics in the black and progressive communities.

Al Sharpton, a sometime rival and sometime supporter of Jackson's, endorsed Fulani's independent presidential bid in 1988. In 1990 he wrote in one of his regular columns in the political weekly *National Alliance* (for which I served as executive editor), "Make no mistake about it," he argued, "the Democratic Party has decided that they will not even attempt to pretend to be liberals.... For this party, after eight years of Jackson candidacies, after I don't know how many conferences on delegate selection and equal representation, can now be controlled by the strong moderate wing that has taken social inequality as its theme and economic inequality as its goal."[7]

In that moment, Sharpton was feeling the billowing constraints of the Democratic Party's control over the black vote. The questions raised but unanswered by the Gary Declaration were now his to grapple with. He decided to push the envelope with Fulani.

Having completed her presidential bid and now concentrating on building national infrastructure for a multiracial independent movement, Fulani undertook her second run for governor of New York. This campaign had a specific, party-building purpose. Fifty thousand votes would give the New Alliance Party (NAP) a permanent line on the ballot. Sharpton, with whom Fulani had marched for racial justice in the earliest days of his civil rights career, endorsed her independent candidacy. He toured Buffalo, Rochester, and Syracuse with her—stumping for her independent candidacy, meeting with newspaper editorial boards and reporters on her behalf. He brought Minister Louis Farrakhan to a press conference at the Grand Hyatt Hotel in New York City to endorse her campaign. On Election Day, Fulani polled 31,000 votes,[8] short of the 50,000 vote requirement to achieve ballot status. Sharpton was starting to recognize something that Fulani already knew. The process of independent politics taking root in the black community would be long, difficult, and uncertain.

Two years later, Sharpton threw his own hat into the ring for the U.S. Senate, using the inside-outside tactic pioneered by the NAP. He posted a candidacy as a Democrat and asked Fulani and Fred Newman to put him on their independent line so he could simultaneously run as an independent—hence, the inside-outside label. Sharpton ultimately withdrew his NAP candidacy under pressure from state Democratic Party leaders, telling the *New York Times*, "I am committed at this point to try to change the Democratic Party. . . . If I see that become impossible then I would go toward a third party. But I clearly stayed away from that this year."[9] Fulani, by contrast, did not. She ran for the presidency again in 1992, which became her springboard into an alliance with the Perot movement, the founding of the Reform Party, and the opportunity to shape a new political partnership for black America.

Given the level of dominance by the Democratic Party in black communities, conventional wisdom held that black voters would be immune to the attractions of political independence. Yet after Rev. Jesse Jackson's historic 1984 presidential run, the Institute for

Social Research at the University of Michigan conducted a survey that showed 57 percent of Jackson's voters would have voted for him as an independent had that been possible.[10] By 1999 the Joint Center for Political and Economic Studies polls found that among African Americans between 18 and 25, 30 percent considered themselves independents.[11] However, yearning for political independence and exercising it are two different things. This was one reason that the mass black exodus from the Democrats in the 2005 New York City mayoral election produced such a strong reaction against the Independence Party from Democratic Party leaders. It was one occasion when black voters exercised their independent power.

In some instances, the institutionalized resistance to liberating African Americans from preordained loyalty to the Democratic Party came perilously close to becoming government policy, as happened after election reform was passed by the voters of Kinston, North Carolina.

In Kinston, where municipal government is dominated by Democrats, voters adopted a 2009 referendum on a system of nonpartisan elections by a margin of 63.8 percent to 36.2 percent. It is estimated that 45–50 percent of black voters backed the initiative. However, since any changes in election law in North Carolina are subject to review, or pre-clearance, by the Justice Department under Section 5 of the Voting Rights Act, the changes mandated by the election results required approval. The Department of Justice (DOJ), acting under its Voting Rights Authority, overturned the election results and nullified the shift to a nonpartisan system. In the decision, Acting Assistant U.S. Attorney General Loretta King wrote:

> Black voters have had limited success in electing candidates of choice during recent municipal elections. The success that they have achieved has resulted from cohesive support for candidates during the Democratic primary . . . It follows, therefore, that the elimination of party affiliation on the ballot will likely reduce the ability of blacks to elect candidates of choice.[12]

From the DOJ's point of view, initially, black voters need the Democratic Party in order to be enfranchised. Ironically, Kinston has an at-large voting system, rather than a single-member district design, which the local Democratic Party has thus far refused to change. Such a change would ensure black representation in the majority black districts, whether Kinston ran on a partisan or a nonpartisan system. But the DOJ did not address that question. Instead, the effort to reduce the influence of the parties (including the Democratic Party) was cast as equivalent to reducing black influence. Subsequently, though, the DOJ announced a reconsideration of its prior position and in February, 2012, withdrew its objections to the nonpartisan system enacted by the voters of Kinston, citing an increase in the size of the black population and in the black share of the electorate.[13]

Interestingly, in the current South Carolina fight to retain open primaries, the clear and present danger for black voters lies in closing the primaries, which black leaders—Democrat and in-dependent—feel would isolate their community by leaving it, un-allied, inside the Democratic Party.

Black political independence has not been an easy road, and not only because the major parties resist it. An all-black party poses real political problems, since black people are a de-mographic minority and need partners to amass political clout on a state or national level. For decades their partners were Democratic Party liberals and labor. But there are limits to the exercise of black power inside the Democratic Party. If the 2008 presidential primaries had been entirely closed to independents, Hillary Clinton, not Barack Obama, would have been the 2008 Democratic nominee.

Independents are rising and many are of color. Exit polling during the Obama campaign picked up on a new trend, manifest for the first time in a number of the Super Tuesday states: the black independent. In Massachusetts 33 percent of African American voters who cast ballots in the Democratic primary self-identified as independents. In Missouri it was 18 percent, Connecticut 22 percent, California 14 percent, New Jersey 13 percent, Georgia 12 percent, in Tennessee 17 percent.

In the end, Obama polled 52 percent of all independent vot-ers, compared with McCain's 44 percent. And in another notable change in the independent demographic, 6 percent of the overall electorate were independents of color—African American, Latino, Asian American, and Native American. Seventy percent of those independent voters chose Barack Obama. It is estimated that more than 20 percent, or one in five, of the independents who voted for Obama on November 4 were people of color.

The black and independent alliance, while risky, has proven itself to be an engine for a progressive and postpartisan vision. Fulani is not the only black progressive leader to attempt to navigate these tricky waters. W.E.B. Du Bois began to build a black base in the Progressive Party in 1912, even while Teddy Roosevelt's chief southern adviser, John Parker, told his presidential candidate that the party "should be a white man's party, recognizing the superior ability of the white man and his superior civilization."[14] In 1924, when another third party was formed which also called itself the Progressive Party, its presidential candidate, Robert La Follette, was denounced as insufficiently aligned on civil rights by the recently formed NAACP. The NAACP advocated independent voting but urged African Americans to boycott the top of the ticket and support only the party's congressional candidates. Going against the black orthodoxy of his time, Du Bois urged a vote for La Follette. He did not believe that La Follette was against civil rights reforms. And, he believed that opposing the two major parties was the most fundamental political point to be made by black voters.

The question of whether white populist and progressive movements would seek out a partnership with black voters and whether black voters would realign themselves outside of the major parties would be tested over and over again, by Du Bois in the first half of the twentieth century and by Fulani at its end.[15]

TEN

UP FOR GRABS

I RECALL VIVIDLY THE MORNING IN MAY 2008, AFTER MORE THAN A YEAR OF POLITICAL drama, when it became apparent to a group of us at the New York offices of IndependentVoting.org that Barack Obama was clinching the Democratic presidential nomination because he had the support of independent voters. Our national networks—using the fusion approach—had mobilized independents for Obama. The results were eye-opening. If primary season voting by independents had been disallowed in 2008, Hillary Clinton would have been the Democratic Party nominee.[1]

Rooted as we were in the complex and turbulent history of the independent movement, this was exciting. But it was also sobering. Independent voters, by then almost 40 percent of the country, had upended a possible Clinton dynasty, giving a black progressive with little Beltway experience the Democratic nomination. They had also lifted up John McCain's flagging campaign in the Republican primaries, making him the GOP nominee. A few months down the road in the general election, independents would break for Obama by eight points. This becoming-organized mass of Americans was searching for radical institutional change.

The estimated 19 million independents who voted for Obama[2] weren't bound by any political party or any ideology. They wanted a new direction for the country. The conventional center/right spin on independents—which stems in part from myths about the Perot decade and in part from the fixation of establishment reformers on finding a political center—would seem to rule out an alliance between independent voters and Obama. But if you'd been *inside* of the process, during the formative years of the independent political movement, it was not a surprise.

Nor was the fact that a majority of independents backed Republicans in the midterm elections two years later. While the postpartisan Obama was elected by independents to be independent (*New York Magazine* called him America's "first Independent president"),[3] he couldn't find a way to make a dent in the embedded partisanship in Washington. Maybe he didn't know how. Those that could have helped him—the progressive wing of the independent movement—were largely ignored. Perhaps the independent movement wasn't big enough, or organized sufficiently, for him to make an appeal to it. Perhaps he couldn't see independents for who they are—a becoming-organized force for a genuinely postpartisan political system. The societal power of the parties, those "sticky" institutions, to use Francis Fukuyama's term, can be overwhelming. Nonetheless, all political leaders and political parties will have to contend with the independents and their search for change—Obama, perhaps, most of all.

As the world heaves itself into the twenty-first century, the marketplace is beginning to devise new strategies for tapping into the huge reserve of nonaligned voters. Will independents aggregate in a third party of some kind? Some argue that they will, others that they must, that the dysfunctionality of the major parties will explode into a new one. The *Wall Street Journal* recently observed that Ross Perot "ran at a moment when 39 percent of Americans said they were dissatisfied with how the nation was being governed. Today, Gallup reports, 81 percent say they are dissatisfied."[4]

The analysts who prognosticate the inevitability of a third party are identifying the existence of a *market* for one. But they are not identifying, or organizing, a social process for creating one. Other than a Perot-style presidential candidacy to galvanize, and fund, a third party (the current favorite to play that part being Mike Bloomberg), the exact means to this end is ambiguous.

One attempt to go beyond this spontaneous-combustion model was Americans Elect, the project initiated by financier Peter Ackerman, founder of Rockport Capital, a forward-looking democracy entrepreneur. Ackerman was an early financial donor to Unity08, created in 2007 by Beltway professionals Doug Bailey, Gerald Rafshoon, and Hamilton Jordan. They had hoped to amass a base of Americans who could propel a third-party presidential candidacy with a national ticket of ideologically divergent candidates for president and vice president. This Unity ticket would "shock the system" back into functionality. Unity08 never achieved the political traction it desired and was hobbled by a Federal Election Commission (FEC) ruling, which categorized it as a political committee and thereby limited financial contributions to the endeavor. Ackerman took over the ill-fated Unity08, led it through litigation against the FEC, won an important decision in the Court of Appeals whereby the FEC was forced to recognize a process, rather than a party or candidacy, and then funded Unity08's political reincarnation as Americans Elect.

Americans Elect fashioned itself as a kind of transitional apparatus—not yet an alternative party, but an alternative nominating process. Ackerman raised the seed money to create ballot lines in all 50 states while erecting an Internet-based platform for voters to participate in nominating the unity presidential ticket. His purpose was to create national unity by superseding the parties' nominating process with a popular alternative. The process failed to identify a candidate.

I first met Ackerman in 2009, after he had already undertaken the litigation but before he had established Americans Elect. We had several lengthy discussions about how to bring this process-based initiative into existence. As Peter told me, and I agreed, the time for abstract or metaphysical complaints about partisanship and the shortcomings of the political system was over. He wanted to act. He was somewhat fearful of the fusion approach of IndependentVoting. org because he thought the major parties would overpower the independents in any kind of partnership. Always a danger, surely. But he thought he could make Americans Elect into a real alternative by creating its ballot status infrastructure and then opening a door to the public to use it to go beyond the two parties.

Ackerman's approach had some interesting features, not least of which was that it responded to partisan dysfunction with a novel process. Still, while it offered an alternative process for nominating a ticket, it set up closely held mechanisms that allowed its founders to control the nomination. And its vision for the ticket stopped short of pressing the need to transform America's political process as a whole. When I asked Peter where a political reform agenda fit into the plan, he suggested that it would come later. Americans Elect spokespeople say that changing the nominating process by taking it outside of the parties will change the way a candidate governs if elected. But even Barack Obama, who was nominated through a partially open process in which independents could vote, and in which independents gave him the nomination, could not overcome the structural partisanship in Washington. Consequently, Americans Elect proffered only a new way of getting to an old place. Put another way, it hoped to use public anger at the parties to promote centrism and restabilize the party system at a time when 40 percent of Americans are moving away from both. Given that the Americans Elect rules tightly controlled the authorization of potential candidates, it intended to determine the nature, the extent, and even the leader of a political revolt—before it even happened.

While Americans Elect projected an alternative to the standard presidential process, it was also, as Al Hunt of Bloomberg News observed, a top-down one.[5] Though *New York Times* columnist Tom Friedman, supporting the Americans Elect approach, points to new technologies from Amazon.com to the iPod as signs that innovations can revolutionize entire industries or sectors,[6] a process innovation that hopes to stabilize an old sector can hardly be considered revolutionary.

The creation of No Labels, a Washington, DC–based group, was prompted by the lack of a mobilizable mass base for bipartisan cooperation. Initiated by Nancy Jacobson, a deft Democratic Party fund-raiser, and Mark McKinnon, an equally deft Republican consultant, No Labels is advancing the proposition that a popular force at the center—in the style of MoveOn.org on the left and the Tea Party on the right—can drive extreme partisanship to the margins. They are invoking the need to restore a sensible center in American politics, but at a time when the horizontal left/center/right paradigm is of shrinking value and the political environment is more and more fragmented. Restoring a "center" rests on the supposition that the existing institutions and power relations can and should be restored. Independents, in contrast, are searching for ways to develop the political system in accord with changing times.

No Labels stumbled recently when it urged supporters in Maine who were registered independents to reregister as Republicans so they could vote for Senator Olympia Snowe in an upcoming Republican primary. The motive was that Snowe is a moderate, targeted by the Tea Party wing of the GOP, and No Labels felt that it should step in to protect those in government who practice bipartisanship. Catana Barnes, the leader of Independent Voters of Nevada, who heard the appeal, resigned her membership in No Labels as a result, telling organizers that under no circumstances should independents be asked to give up their independence. Word of Barnes's resignation spread quickly through IndependentVoting.org's networks and was loudly applauded. Ironically enough, Senator Snowe later announced that she would not seek reelection because Congress had become too partisan for her to function effectively.

Independents, organized without being a third party, are battling for structural reforms that will loosen the grip of parties on government and politics. This is a long-term approach, one that focuses as much on the development of the movement as it does on correcting the ills of the partisan arrangement. Those two, development and democratization, go hand in hand, or neither will go anywhere at all. Surely, the competition among organized forces in the independent movement will become more intense in the decades to come.

In November 2009, just days after the anti-party New York City Independence Party polled a record-breaking 150,000 votes for Mike Bloomberg, while elsewhere in the country independents showed up at the polls and voted for Republican candidates—a bellwether of the protest to come in 2010—I had a conversation with Fred Newman about these events. Every week, from 2005 until he became too ill to do so, we watched the Sunday morning talk shows and discussed them. These conversations were transcribed and published as a weekly on-line commentary called *Talk/Talk*, which was read by tens of thousands of independents nationwide for six years.

I remembered a particular *Talk/Talk* recently while writing *Independents Rising*, as it dealt with the relationship between organizing the independent movement and the unorganized movement of Americans en masse away from the parties—which is, ultimately, the subject of this book. Though it's impossible to sum up the movement—how can you sum up something that is in its earliest stages of development and self-definition?—this *Talk/Talk* conversation was about how the movement is up for grabs. Here's a section of this exchange.

> NEWMAN: Unlike the way these traditional pundits see it, the independent vote is up for grabs—from an *organizing* point of view. And, it's the *organized* independents which are a major factor.... The punditocracy's analysis doesn't know from organized and unorganized. That's not one of their categories. They don't understand the meaning of the process of grassroots organizing, of something "becoming."
>
> SALIT: I buy that completely.
>
> NEWMAN: There's a methodological error in the way that they report, for the most part. They want to speak of the independents,

of what the independents are doing, but the way that they define independents is solely on the basis of who they vote for.

SALIT: Correct.

NEWMAN: So, there's a contradiction there, because they don't identify independents as anything other than the way they vote. So, then, what is the meaning of the sentence *The independents voted this way,* if, on the pundits' definition independents *are* who they vote for.

SALIT: Why bother to call them independents at all?

NEWMAN: They don't believe in the concept of independents having independent existence. And that means they don't believe in the process of independents becoming organized. That's why they never cover that. They don't think it will turn into anything unless a Ross Perot comes along and turns it into something. They don't see anything separate from that.

SALIT: We're organizing on the ground as rapidly as we can. My experience is that there's so much out there to be organized. And, when I think about Obama, I think, if our movement were bigger, not just bigger quantitatively, but if it had more power, he would have something to go up against the Democratic Party with.

NEWMAN: I don't even know if the conditional language of "if it had more power" makes sense.

SALIT: Because?

NEWMAN: Because I don't know what "it" is and I don't know what "power" is in this context. Look, you have what you have. That's what you have. And you organize what you have. . . . When I say I don't know what "it" is, I mean that it's still very embryonic, very new. And it's emerging at the rate that it's emerging at. And it does the things that it does. So, when you say that they're looking for trends, that's not quite accurate. They're looking for trends which they take to be comprehensible and possible, but only from a two-party point of view.

SALIT: True enough.

NEWMAN: So, they're not looking at trends at all. They won't look at *our* trends. They're not even looking at trends in the same way that we consider trends. We know that there are two dominant major parties. But we also know that there's something else going on. It's a "becoming," if you will. . . . And they don't consider that when they analyze what the elections are all about. It's all swing, swing, swing, swing. Last year they swung one way. This year they swung another. Well, what if what you're calling a "swing" is the emergence of a new kind of political movement?

SALIT: I'd say it is . . .

NEWMAN: Correct, and it's a misnomer to call it a third-party movement. It's as much an *anti-party* movement as anything, at this point in that process. . . . History includes having a way of understanding history. I think what I'm describing is a closer characterization of what's going on than simply the cyclical swing of a bloc of voters. And this means there is an historical, logical dilemma for these pundits. In some respects, they can't or won't or are not allowed to think in these terms.

SALIT: I assume if they do, they'll be out of a job.

NEWMAN: They only can see things in terms of parties . . . and it makes sense. I'm not saying they're wrong or they've been brainwashed. I'm saying that's just what has happened. George Washington was against parties from the start.

SALIT: Yes.

NEWMAN: But no sooner had Washington spoken out against parties than four years later we had the dirtiest, most partisan election in the history of the United States of America. . . . He was trying to fight the anti-party fight and he lost, cold. And the parties took over, boom. And they've been entrenched for well over 200 years.

SALIT: But that is going through a transformation.

NEWMAN: Yes. But you don't so easily see transformations because most of the "looking" is based on what was there before. As radicals, we're trying to see this whole process, not abstractly, but while reorganizing it, from the vantage point of where we believe it's heading. . . . That's why, in this age of super advanced technology, I'm still a believer in grassroots organizing.

SALIT: Me, too. . . . This is why, as I told you, the exchange I had with a reporter at the *New York Times* really made me laugh. In a fairly succinct way I put in front of him a summary of the New York City results, and what, by any standard, was a momentous new development in the history of minor parties and in the performance of independent voters. It is, after all, a climate in which everyone is saying, *It's all about the indepen-dents.* I got back a one-line response that said, "I put it in, but they cut it." I broke out laughing!

NEWMAN: Disposed of by the stroke of a pen!

SALIT: Or a "delete" button.[7]

In his Farewell Address in 1796, George Washington warned that political parties can "become potent engines by which cunning, ambitious and unprincipled men will be enabled to subvert the power of the people, and to usurp for themselves the reins of government."[8] The American people want that power back. The question is how to get it back.

The independent political movement faces very difficult growth challenges that will not be resolved in or by the 2012 elections. If anything, the economic crisis and the uncertainties it produces will prolong the life of the old order, not accelerate the progress toward a new one. Independent politics is, after all, an effort to introduce a new culture of politics, using tools of the old order while creating new ones along the way. That is the nature of the struggle for a post-partisan America.

ACKNOWLEDGMENTS

IN EARLY 2010 I HAD WHAT TURNED OUT TO BE A PROPITIOUS LUNCH. JOSH ROSNER, the coauthor of *Reckless Endangerment* and an enthusiastic and loyal supporter of independent politics, introduced me to Serena Jones, his editor at Henry Holt. Over fried artichokes and orzo, the three of us spent two hours discussing the rise of independent voters and the changing chemistry of American politics. Serena introduced me to Robert Guinsler at Sterling Lord Literistic, whose energy for the project made me confident I could write this story. Robert found me the perfect match at Palgrave Macmillan. My editor, Emily Carleton, took my somewhat rough-hewn narrative and gave it a good shine, never once asking me to soft-pedal or low-key anything. When you are an outsider in the mainstream political world, you become accustomed to being asked (or told) to "cool it" or "clean it up." Emily respected the real history of this movement, and she trusted my passion for telling it. More than once she sent me back a chapter covering some serious affront to independents with a note about how she couldn't believe how raw it was. That helped keep me going. Her team, especially Laura Lancaster and Alan Bradshaw, was great to work with.

My agent, Robert Guinsler, was also struck by some of the resistance to independent politics. From our very first conversation, he felt that the story of a movement-in-the-making, rooted in 40 percent of the American public, was very worthy. His perseverance and good humor made it happen.

I was incredibly fortunate to have John Opdycke—who is also the chief fund-raiser for IndependentVoting.org—as my go-to guy for all phases of the writing. He headed a crack team of researchers who focused like a laser on a very compressed timetable. David Belmont, Sarah Lyons, Christina Putz, and Lauren Ross did an amazing job. Nancy Hanks of *The Hankster*, Bob Conroy, and my assistant Caroline Donnola added to their tonnage. In addition to her research role, Lauren Ross assembled the manuscript and managed all the footnotes, endnotes, and sources.

Many friends and colleagues took this journey with me. I am so lucky to be part of a broad community of people who were rooting for me and this project. To mention just a few—when I asked Richard Sokolow to help get the deal started, he worked the phones on my behalf. Harry Kresky helped me crystallize the framing of some key aspects of the book. So did Cathy Stewart, Michael Lewis, Jason Olson, Wayne Griffin, Lois Holzman, Gwen Mandell, Nancy Ross, Omar Ali, Lenora Fulani, and Phyllis Goldberg. Many others, notably Alvaader Frazier, Cathy Salit, Murray and Susan Salit, Kathy Fiess, Linda Curtis, Doug Balder, Christine LaCerva, and

Elizabeth Newman were so giving with their moral support. Kim Svoboda was there at the start and at the finish, as she unfailingly is. Gabrielle Kurlander, always a special friend, helped me through the difficult early weeks of writing which were filled with sadness for both of us. Chris Street was unwavering during that time, providing large amounts of solace and vodka.

I began working on *Independents Rising* in June 2011, a few weeks before Fred Newman, a major character in this story and in every aspect of my life, passed away. Just a few days before he died, as his health was demonstrably failing, I told him about the outline I'd written, the boxes I'd filled with source material, the charts I'd made to create the narrative. I hadn't yet put pen to paper, but I was babbling on about all I planned to do. He looked at me with a quintessential Newman grimace, but not without tenderness. "Write words," he said. So I did.

Lastly, I am grateful to the many, many unsung independents who are the pioneers of this movement. I hope I've brought some small light to our cause.

NOTES

INTRODUCTION

1. Charlie Cook, "The Cook Report: Trend or Fluke?" *National Journal*, March 10, 2011.
2. In 1995, Colorado Governor Richard Lamm convened "The Lamm Group" to promote the idea of (and philosophy for) a centrist third party and to explore the possibilities of fielding a candidate in 1996. Other members of the group included Senator Bill Bradley, Democrat of New Jersey; Lowell P. Weicker, Jr., a former Republican senator and independent governor from Connecticut; Senator Paul Tsongas, Democrat of Massachusetts; former Senator Gary Hart, Democrat of Colorado; former Representative Tim Penny, Democrat of Minnesota; and Governor Angus King, the independent governor of Maine.
3. Edison Media Research, Nov. 7, 2006.
4. Research Department, Committee for a Unified Independent Party; compilation of exit poll data gathered by Edison Media Research during the 2008 presidential primaries.
5. Edison Media Research, Nov. 4, 2008.
6. Of the self-identified independents who voted in the 2008 New Hampshire Republican presidential primary, 40 percent voted for McCain and 27 percent voted for Romney. McCain won the New Hampshire primary with 37 percent of the vote. Romney finished second with 32 percent. Since independents comprised 37 percent of the total voters in that primary, McCain's support from independents accounted for virtually all of his five-point margin of victory over Romney. (Edison Media Research, Jan. 8, 2008.)
7. Edison Media Research, Nov. 2, 2010.
8. Gordon S. Wood, *The Idea of America: Reflections on the Birth of the United States* (New York: Penguin Press, 2011), 48.
9. Diane Cardwell, "Political Party of Outsiders Has Come in from the Cold," *New York Times*, Aug. 27, 2002.
10. Jeffrey M. Jones, "Democratic Party ID Drops in 2010, Tying 22-Year Low," Gallup, Jan. 5, 2011, http://www.gallup.com/poll/145463/democratic-party-drops-2010-tying-year-low.aspx.

CHAPTER ONE

1. Arnold J. Toynbee, *A Study of History: Abridgment of Volumes I-VI by D.C. Somervell* (Oxford, England: Oxford University Press, 1946), 369.

2. William Greider, *One World, Ready or Not: The Manic Logic of Global Capitalism* (New York: Simon & Schuster, 1997), 212.

3. "The People, The Press & Politics: The New Political Landscape," Pew Research Center for the People & the Press, Sept. 21, 1994.

4. Initiative and Referendum Institute at the University of Southern California, http://www.iandrinstitute.org/Colorado.htm.

5. The article was later expanded into a book by Fukuyama, *The End of History and the Last Man* (New York: Free Press, 1992).

6. Francis Fukuyama, "The End of History?" *National Interest,* Summer 1989.

7. Andrew Kopkind, *The Thirty Years' Wars: Dispatches and Diversions of a Radical Journalist, 1965-1994,* ed. Joann Wypijewski (London: Verso Books, 1995), 471.

8. Gordon S. Black and Benjamin D. Black, *The Politics of American Discontent: How a New Party Can Make Democracy Work Again* (New York: John Wiley & Sons, 1994), 113.

9. Andrew Kopkind and Alexander Cockburn, "Democrats, Perot, and the Left," *Nation,* July 20-27, 1992, 86.

10. "The $642,000 Longshot," *New York Daily News,* Dec. 28, 1991.

11. *Concord Monitor* article, Dec. 30, 1991, quoted in Lenora Fulani, *The Making of a Fringe Candidate 1992* (New York: Castillo International, 1992), 1.

12. Brown served as the 34th governor of California (1975–1983) and sought the Democratic nomination for president of the United States in 1992. He is currently serving as the 39th California governor (2011–present).

13. Dan Friedman and Phyllis Goldberg, "Leaderless Group Scabs on Fulani Democracy Picket," *National Alliance,* Jan. 30, 1992.

14. Bill Clinton, *My Life* (New York: Alfred A. Knopf, 2004), 401-2.

15. *Larry King Live,* CNN, Feb. 20, 1992.

16. Clinton, *My Life,* 419.

17. Kopkind and Cockburn, "The Democrats, Perot, and the Left," 81.

18. Fulani polled under 100,000 votes, less than her quarter million votes in 1988. The total number of votes for third-party presidential candidates other than Perot dropped by 30 percent in 1992 as compared to 1988.

19. *Washington Post,* summary of exit polls conducted by Voter Research and Surveys on Election Day, Nov. 3, 1992, http://www.washingtonpost.com/wp-srv/politics/interactives/independents/data-party-identification.html.

20. Roper Center, University of Connecticut, summary of exit polls conducted by Voter Research and Surveys on Election Day, Nov. 3, 1992, http://www.roper center.uconn.edu/elections/how_groups_voted/voted_92.html#.Ttbc8GP0vZJ.

21. Voter News Service exit poll, reported in the *New York Times,* Nov. 10, 1996, http://www.nytimes.com/1996/11/10/weekinreview/forget-the-gender-gap-what-about-the-smoker-.gap.html?pagewanted=print&src=pm&gwh=A8840D74AB2BD70555D5E72322C2CC93.

22. Al From and Will Marshall, "The Road to Realignment: Democrats and Perot Voters," Democratic Leadership Council, 1993, http://www.dlc.org/ndol_ci.cfm?contentid=2446&kaid=127&subid=269.

CHAPTER TWO

1. Gerald L. Posner, *Citizen Perot: His Life and Times* (New York: Random House, 1996), 322.

2. Ibid., 325.

3. In his book *The Politics of American Discontent: How a New Party Can Make Democracy Work Again*, Dr. Black projected the base of a new party as mainly white and politically moderate. He did not believe black and other traditional left/liberal Democratic Party constituencies would break away to be part of a new electoral coalition. Further, he argued that black voters should support a break away by other elements of the Democratic Party because it would make them a more powerful force in the machinery left behind:

   > African Americans are more likely to believe in the continuation of the two-party system, which is logical given their bloc support of the Democratic Party. However, if one considers the situation strategically, it is ironically in the best interest of minorities to advocate the creation of a new party because it would most likely increase the minorities' power within the Democratic Party. Assuming a percentage of moderate Democrats would defect to a moderate third party, the influence of the minorities, who would make up a larger share of the remaining Democratic Party activists, would increase proportionally. (pp. 155-156)

4. In 1992 the left-wing *Nation* magazine published an article critical of Fulani's independent presidential campaign under the sensationalistic headline "The New Alliance Party—Dr. Fulani's Snake-Oil Show." This piece and a negative "research report" by a left investigative group written during her 1988 presidential campaign titled "Clouds Blur the Rainbow" became the bible of anti-Fulani and anti-Newman talking points. For a more thorough treatment of the controversy, see "Fred Newman and His Critics," http:www.frednewmanphd.com/newmans-critics.html.

5. Gregory Curtis, "Threat or Menace," *Texas Monthly*, 20:8, Aug. 1992.

6. Nicholas Sabatine III, "Patriot Party Second Annual Convention, C-SPAN," May 20, 1995.

7. Jack W. Germond, "Jackson Steals Opening of Perot's Conference by Defending Independents' Role," *Baltimore Sun*, Aug. 12, 1995.

8. Ibid.

9. Scott Pendleton, "Perot Army Seeks Change, Double Time," *Christian Science Monitor*, Aug. 14, 1995.

10. Ibid.

11. Though Black and Fulani had fallen out over the Patriot Party founding in April 1994, he reached out several months later and asked her to join him in founding the Independence Party of New York.

12. B. Drummond Ayres Jr., "Perot Is Starting a 3d-Party Drive," *New York Times*, Sept. 26, 1995, http://select.nytimes.com/gst/abstract.html?res=F60615FC3B540 C758EDDA00894DD494D81&scp=2&sq=%22Perot%20is%20Starting%20a%20 3d-Party%20Drive%22&st=cse.

13. American Independent Party (AIP) became a ballot-status party in California in 1968 when Alabama Governor George Wallace, a segregationist, left the Democratic Party to run for president as an independent.

14. Rogers Worthington, "California Gives Perot Until Friday," *Chicago Tribune*, Oct. 5, 1995.

15. Frank Bruni, "Perot and Populist Group See Benefits in an Alliance," *New York Times*, Aug. 21, 1996.

16. Michael Kelly, "After the First Date," *New Yorker*, April 22, 1996.

17. Richard D. Lamm and Gary Imhoff, *The Immigration Time Bomb: The Fragmenting of America* (New York: Truman Talley Books, 1985).

18. In 1986, while running for governor in New York, Fulani was called upon by then Governor Mario Cuomo to repudiate Minister Louis Farrakhan as a condition for her participation in the gubernatorial debates. Fulani refused, citing her many differences with Farrakhan while asserting that repudiating another black leader was tantamount to repudiating the black community, something she "would never, ever do." In 1988, after a series of discussions with Fulani, Farrakhan and the Nation of Islam briefly dabbled with the idea of becoming political independents. In 1990, he endorsed Fulani's second gubernatorial run at a press conference organized by Rev. Al Sharpton. But Farrakhan never made the break. The Million Man March featured an array of Democratic Party elected officials. Fulani was not invited.

19. Ernest Tollerson, "Politics: Third Party; Perot's Committee Refuses to Give Rival the List of Reform Party Supporters," *New York Times*, July 23, 1996, http://www .nytimes.com/1996/07/23/us/politics-third-party-perot-s-committee-refuses -give-rival-list-reform-party.html?scp=1&sq=%22Perot's%20committee%20 refuses%20to%20Give%20Rival%20the%20List%22&st=cse.

20. Laurence I. Barrett, "Campaign '96: A Real Candidate or Perot's Sacrificial Lamm?" *Time*, July 15, 1996, http://www.time.com/time/magazine/article/0,9171,984831,00.html.

21. "Fixing the Reform Party," editorial, *New York Times*, July 24, 1996.

CHAPTER THREE

1. In addition to his deep involvement in independent politics, Newman was also a playwright and lyricist. He authored 50 plays and musicals. The score for *Sally and Tom: The American Way* was created by the Grammy Award-winning composer Annie Roboff, Newman's frequent collaborator.

2. The Minnesota Independence Party changed its name, for a time, to the Minnesota Reform Party.

3. Fred Newman and Lois Holzman, *The End of Knowing: A New Developmental Way of Learning* (London: Routledge, 1997), 32.

4. Matt Bai, "The Outlaws Come to Town," *Newsweek*, Sept. 26, 1999. © 1999, The Newsweek/Daily Beast Company LLC. All rights reserved. Used by permission and protected by the Copyright Laws of the United States. The printing, copying, redistribution, or retransmission of the Material without express written permission is prohibited.

5. *Hardball with Chris Matthews*, NBC, Sept. 23, 1999.

6. *Inside Politics*, CNN, Oct. 26, 1999.

7. Ibid.

8. *CNN & Company*, CNN, Oct. 25, 1999.

9. Bruce Shapiro, "Buchanan-Fulani: New Team?" *Nation*, Oct. 14, 1999.

10. National Press Club, Washington, DC, Nov. 11, 1999, http://www.c-spanvideo. org/program/153554-1.

11. "Fulani Endorses Buchanan," Editorial, *Wall Street Journal*, Nov. 12, 1999.

12. Though Buchanan supporters attempted to rig the online primary, violating the rules promulgated by the Reform Party's Presidential Nominating Committee, and then voted at a split convention to nullify the results of the primary by overriding them, the Federal Election Commission (FEC) still recognized Buchanan as the Reform Party nominee and awarded him the treasury. In making its determination, the FEC ignored the national party process altogether and instead determined that the first contender to be certified on the ballot in ten states (between Buchanan and Natural Law presidential candidate John Hagelin, who became the anti-Buchanan candidate), would get the money.

CHAPTER FOUR

1. "Retro-Politics: The Political Typology: Version 3.0," Pew Research Center for the People & the Press, Nov. 11, 1999.

2. Ibid.

3. John McCaslin, "Inside the Beltway," *Washington Times*, Dec. 2, 2003.

4. New York State Board of Elections, General Election Vote, Nov. 8, 1994.

5. Diane Cardwell, "Political Party of Outsiders Has Come in from the Cold," *New York Times*, Aug. 27, 2002.

6. Democrat Sal Albanese, who lost the Democratic primary for mayor in 1997, was the IP's mayoral candidate that year, but in deference to the Democratic nominee, Ruth Messinger, did not campaign at all. Giuliani won overwhelmingly.

7. New York State Board of Elections, General Election Vote, Nov. 3, 1998.

8. In 1999, while her husband was president, Clinton had travelled to the West Bank where she met and embraced the wife of PLO leader Yasser Arafat. A photo of this encounter had been widely circulated, to the consternation of the Clinton camp since it opened her to charges of being sympathetic to the Palestinian cause.

9. George Stephanopoulos on *This Week with Sam and Cokie*, ABC, April 30, 2000.

10. During the 1992 campaign, candidate Bill Clinton appeared at Rev. Jesse Jackson's Rainbow Coalition conference and unexpectedly criticized a young female rapper, Sister Souljah. The speech was widely regarded as Clinton's delivering a "coded message" to white voters that, unlike other white Democrats, he would not be soft on the black community.

11. Joel Siegel, "Hil Looks Left for a Fight Now That Rudy's Ill," *New York Daily News*, May 2, 2000.

12. Rev. Al Sharpton, guest editorial, "Lenora Fulani Is No Anti-Semite," *New York Amsterdam News*, May 10, 2000.

13. Eric Fettmann, "Hillary Does Right—Rudy Should Have Zapped Fulani & Buchanan, Too," *New York Post*, May 3, 2000.

14. "Rudy Giuliani's Cancer: Will He Still Run for Senate?" *Crossfire*, CNN, May 1, 2000.

15. Cathy Stewart [chair of the New York County Independence Party], interview with the author, Aug. 27, 2011.

16. Press statement: Laureen Oliver, Independence Party founder, State Secretary, May 8, 2000. In 2000, Donald Trump paid the legal fees of embattled Independence

Party chair Jack Essenberg in an effort to prevent the party's rank and file from electing a new chair and democratizing the party's rules.

17. Michael Tomasky, *Hillary's Turn: Inside Her Improbable, Victorious Senate Campaign* (New York: Free Press, 2001), 161.

18. The Natural Law Party was formed by practitioners of Transcendental Meditation. Dr. John Hagelin, a quantum physicist, was their presidential candidate.

CHAPTER FIVE

1. Eric Lipton, "Waxing Philosophic, and Just Waxing, in 9-Hour Term-Limit Hearing," *New York Times*, March 9, 2001.

2. As mayor, Bloomberg and the City Council abrogated the term limits law in 2008, when he sought a third term.

3. In 2001, there were 699,190 unaffiliated voters and 51,981 IP enrollees in New York City, a total of 751,171. This figure was 18.3 percent of the 4,104,923 total registered voters in New York City. (Source: New York State Board of Elections, Nov. 1, 2001 Enrollment Report.)

4. In 2001, he faced off against Herman Badillo, another convert to the GOP from the Democratic Party, to win the Republican primary.

5. In 2001, there were 2,748,538 Democrats as compared to 523,761 Republicans in New York City, a ratio of 5.2 to 1. (Source: New York State Board of Elections, Nov. 1, 2001 Enrollment Report.)

6. Rudy Giuliani received 62,469 votes on the Liberal Party line in 1993. His margin of victory was 53,340 votes. (Source: New York City Board of Elections, General Election Vote, Nov. 2, 1993.) The Democrats, with a long history of support from the Liberal Party, were furious at the abandonment. The Liberals reached their heyday in the Giuliani administration, but through a combination of corruption scandals and political misjudgments, the Liberal Party lost ballot status in 2002.

7. Walter Karp, *Indispensable Enemies: The Politics of Misrule in America* (New York: Franklin Square Press, 1993), 20-21.

8. Adam Nagourney, "Bloomberg Says Elections Should Be Nonpartisan," *New York Times*, June 8, 2001.

9. Lenora Fulani, "Why I'm Endorsing Mike Bloomberg for Mayor," *Black Star News*, June 21–27, 2001.

10. Cedric Muhammad, "Dr. Lenora Fulani, Michael Bloomberg and Making the Black Vote 'Unpredictable,'" *BlackElectorate.com*, July 26, 2001.

11. Wilbert A. Tatum, "I've Got Money . . . Elect Me and I Will Give You Some," *New York Amsterdam News*, July 19, 2001.

12. Joel Siegel, "Bloomberg Is Courting Fulani Party," *New York Daily News*, April 19, 2001.

13. Michael Bloomberg, "Get Party Politics Out of City Hall," *New York Newsday*, July 17, 2001.

14. Judith Hope, "A Place for Parties," *New York Newsday*, July 31, 2001.

15. Douglas E. Schoen, *The Political Fix: Changing the Game of American Democracy, From the Grass Roots to the White House* (New York: Times Books/ Henry Holt, 2010), 6.

16. Adam Nagourney, "Ferrer Formally Concedes to Green in a Democratic Show of Unity," *New York Times*, Oct. 20, 2001, http://www.nytimes.com/2001/10/20 /nyregion/ferrer-formally-concedes-to-green-in-a-democratic-show-of-unity

.html?scp=1&sq=%22Ferrer%20Formally%20Concedes%20to%20Green%20
in%20a%20Democratic%20Show%20of%20Unity%22&st=cse.
17. Source: New York City Board of Elections, General Election Vote, Nov. 6, 2001.
18. Source: Edison Media Research, Nov. 6, 2001.
19. Source: New York City Board of Elections, General Election Vote, Nov. 6, 2001.
20. Joel Siegel, "Our Votes Gave Mike Win: Fulani," *New York Daily News*, Nov. 9, 2001.
21. Robert Hardt, Jr., "Mike Raps 'Backer' Fulani's Message," *New York Post*, Sept. 20, 2001.
22. Michael Saul, "Independence Suit Says Fight Puts Line in Doubt," *New York Daily News*, Oct. 4, 2001.
23. Upon taking office, Bloomberg asked and the state legislature agreed to give the mayor control over the New York City public schools, a first step in Bloomberg's promised reform of the system.
24. Kirsten Danis and Frankie Edozien, "'Party'-Pooping Bloomy Wants Non-Partisan Voting," *New York Post*, June 18, 2002.
25. Julia Levy, "Skeptics Weigh in at Charter Hearing," *New York Sun*, July 26, 2002.
26. Karp, *Indispensable Enemies*, 20.
27. "Mayor Mike Pays an Ugly Debt," editorial, *New York Post*, July 15, 2002.
28. Benjamin Smith, "New Flap Over Fulani Lawyer," *New York Sun*, July 15, 2002.
29. Harry Kresky to Mayor Bloomberg, letter dated July 30, 2002.
30. People's Coalition for Nonpartisan Municipal Elections press conference, Aug. 1, 2002.
31. Citizens Union designates candidates as "preferred."
32. Francis S. Barry, *The Scandal of Reform: The Grand Failures of New York's Political Crusaders and the Death of Nonpartisanship* (New Brunswick, NJ: Rutgers University Press, 2009), 136.
33. Jennifer Steinhauer, "Charter Revision Opponents Prepare to Battle Bloomberg," *New York Times*, July 19. 2002, http://www.nytimes.com/2002/07/19/nyregion/charter-revision-opponents-prepare-to-battle-bloomberg.html.
34. "The Charter Revision Addiction," editorial, *New York Times*, July 9, 2002.
35. *The City in Transition: Interim Succession and the Mayoralty*, Report of the New York City Charter Revision Commission, Sept. 3, 2002.
36. Jennifer Steinhauer, "Party Assigns Itself Blame Over Inaction on Charter," *New York Times*, Aug. 31, 2002.
37. "Rangel on Bloomberg," editorial, *New York Sun*, July 8, 2003.
38. "Ferrer, Gartner Square Off on Election Proposal," editorial, *Newsday*, Sept. 21, 2003.
39. Greg Sargent, "E Pluribus Dems," *New York Magazine*, Nov. 23, 2003.
40. Stephanie Gaskell, "Minority Pols Rip Nonpartisan Plan," *New York Daily News*, Oct. 29, 2003.
41. Jennifer Steinhauer, "Mayor Details Plan to Revise City Elections," *New York Times*, July 18, 2003.
42. Eric Wolff, "Four Presidential Candidates Oppose Nonpartisan Push," *New York Sun*, Oct. 30, 2003.
43. Curtis Taylor, "Coalition Starts Drive to End Party Primaries," *Newsday*, Oct. 7, 2003.
44. Adam Cataldo, "Non-Partisan Elections Get Police, Firefighter Support," *New York Sun*, Oct. 7, 2003.

45. Barry, *The Scandal of Reform*, 208.
46. "Time to Unplug Machine Politics," editorial, *New York Daily News*, July 2, 2003, http://articles.nydailynews.com/2003-07-02/news/18235518_1_nonpartisan -elections-mayor-bloomberg-democratic-party.
47. John P. Avlon, "Vote Yes on Nonpartisan Elections," *New York Sun*, Nov. 3, 2003.
48. "All the Politicians Are Against It: Hello?" editorial, *New York Observer*, Nov. 3, 2003.
49. Barry, *The Scandal of Reform*, 134.
50. Prime voters in New York City are registered Democrats who vote in each and every primary and general election. They represent approximately 6 percent of registered voters and 10 percent of registered Democrats, and they are frequently the only voters who are called or mailed to during a local Democratic Party primary.
51. Gracie Mansion is the New York City mayor's residence, located on the Upper East Side of Manhattan. Mayor Bloomberg has never lived at Gracie Mansion during his three terms. He uses Gracie Mansion for meetings and public functions.
52. Dina Temple-Raston, "Ferrer Forms a Committee as Democrats Exult at Vote," *New York Sun*, Nov. 6, 2003.
53. New York City Board of Elections, General Election Vote, Nov. 4, 2003.

CHAPTER SIX

1. Harry Kresky, "Advisory Opinion Request 2002-01," letter to Federal Election Commission, Jan. 2, 2002.
2. Ibid.
3. Federal Election Commission, "Advisory Opinion Request 2002-01," letter to Harry Kresky, March 8, 2002.
4. Nicholas Lemann, "The Controller," *New Yorker*, May 12, 2003.
5. IndependentVoting.org National Conference, "The Power of Fusion," January 16–17, 2005, New York City.
6. ChIP reached out to the Bush campaign, and the campaign responded with a letter indicating interest in the ChIP process but never followed up. Meanwhile, the vast majority of grassroots independents polled in the ChIP process rejected the Bush option.
7. General Wesley Clark sent a rep to the national ChIP conference but otherwise did not participate.
8. The California recall election took place on October 7, 2003. The ballot consisted of two questions; voters could vote on one or the other, or on both. The first question asked whether Governor Gray Davis should be recalled. If a majority voted no, then the second question would become irrelevant and Davis would remain California's governor. If a majority voted yes, then Davis would be removed from office once the vote was certified, and the second question would determine his successor. Over 55 percent (55.4) voted in favor of recall. Among those voting on the potential replacement, Arnold Schwarzenegger received 48.6 percent of the vote, surpassing Lt. Gov. Cruz Bustamante who received 31.5 percent. (Source: California Secretary of State, http://www.sos.ca.gov/elections/sov/2003_special/.)
9. Stephanie Gaskell and Stefan C. Friedman, "Flip-flop Dean Rips No-Party Vote," *New York Post*, Oct. 30, 2003.

10. Michael R. Blood, "Dean Flip-flops on Bloomy's Ballot," *New York Daily News,* Oct. 30, 2003, http://articles.nydailynews.com/2003-10-30/news/18237276_1_howard -dean-mayor-bloomberg-nonpartisan-elections.

11. Associated Press, "Dean: America Not Safer After Saddam's Capture," *FoxNews. com,* Dec. 16, 2003, http://www.foxnews.com/story/0,2933,105789,00.html.

12. February 21, 2004, New York City, Letter from Fred Newman to Ralph Nader via facsimile.

13. Theresa Amato, *Grand Illusion: The Myth of Voter Choice in a Two-Party Tyranny* (New York: New Press, 2009), 88.

CHAPTER SEVEN

1. Quinnipiac University poll, June 9, 2004.

2. Cliff Hocker, "A Shift from the Left: Study Shows Blacks Drifting from Democratic Party (Washington Report)," *Black Enterprise,* May 1, 2003, http://www.blacken-terprise.com/2003/05/01/a-shift-from-the-left/.

3. Maggie Haberman, "Fulani Factor Faces Mike at Reform Fete," *New York Daily News,* Dec. 3, 2004.

4. Jill Gardiner, "Mayor Accepts Independence Party Award But Maintains Distance," *New York Sun,* Dec. 7, 2004.

5. Jennifer Steinhauer, "Bloomberg Criticizes Parties in Bid for Independence Line," *New York Times,* Dec. 7, 2004.

6. Penn Schoen Berland was the firm that created the database in 2005 for the mayor. What is notable is the depth and breadth of the information collected: political variables such as voting record and donor history, economic data, extensive de-mographics, and lifestyle variables. As Penn Schoen Berland described it on their website: "In 2005 we created PSB's microtargeting segmentation, which we have used successfully for such clients as New York City Mayor Michael Bloomberg." (www.psbresearch.com)

7. Harlem machine refers to the political clubhouse based in Harlem that has influenced African American politics from the 1920s to the present.

8. "New York City Race for Mayor," WNBC/Marist Poll, Sept. 27, 2005, http://maristpoll.marist.edu/wp-content/misc/nycpolls/MY050927.pdf.

9. "New York City Race for Mayor," WNBC/Marist Poll, Oct. 12, 2005, http://marist-poll.marist.edu/wp-content/misc/nycpolls/MY051012.pdf.

10. "As I sat and listened I saw more deeply in Fred's teaching the historical pitfalls of nationalism. After all, according to nationalistic ideology, the Jewish people have gotten the ultimate—land, in the form of a nation state. The fact is, however, that they had to sell their souls to acquire Israel and are required to do the dirtiest work of capitalism—to function as mass murderers of people of color—in order to keep it. Not only that, most of the Jewish people have not benefited from this 'victory.'" (Lenora Fulani, "Always Room for Fulani: Fulani Reviews 'No Room for Zion,'" *National Alliance,* Nov. 16, 1989.)

11. For all the charges of anti-Semitism and divisiveness leveled against Fulani, Newman, and the IP by the Anti-Defamation League (ADL) and others, the de-tractors failed to peel away voters or to disrupt this independent Black/Jewish coalition. Bloomberg polled 70 percent of the Jewish vote and 47 percent of the black vote. (Edison Media Research, Nov. 8, 2005.)

12. "The situation in the Middle East at that time was extremely tense and polarized. Thousands of lives had already been lost on both sides. Few imagined that it could have gotten worse. But it has. At the time, the Israelis were, to my eyes, intransigent with respect to recognition of the Palestinians and support for a two-state solution. I viewed the Israelis as the aggressors and the Palestinians as a colonized people subject to outside authority and occupation. My comments reflected my feelings about the situation during that time. I felt it important to stand up for the people I thought were singularly oppressed. The language I used was harsh and today I would call it excessive. But, even at the time, I never intended to be hurtful to anyone, and never intended to express anything demeaning or derogatory to Jewish people here or in Israel.

"Much has happened since the time I wrote those words. Much killing and murder has taken place on both sides. The situation has become increasingly unstable and dangerous for all involved–whether Palestinian or Israeli. The stand-off has given way to more violence, more disillusionment and more disintegration. My views have changed as part of that process. I do not view Israel as an aggressor. The tragedy is a tragedy for Jew and Arab alike.

"In light of that, I am repudiating my remarks of 18 years ago. They do not express my feelings and deep concerns about the situation in the Middle East. I disassociate myself from them." (Statement by Lenora Fulani at a press conference on the steps of City Hall, Aug. 9, 2008.)

13. *MacKay v. Mandell,* 2006 N.Y. Misc. LEXIS 2330, at 6 (Sup. Ct. NY Co. 2006).

14. "New Yorkers Approve of Mayor More than 3-1 Quinnipiac University Poll Finds; But Most Won't Vote for Him as President." Quinnipiac Polling, Nov. 14, 2006, http://www.quinnipiac.edu/x1302.xml?ReleaseID=984.

15. "The Independence Charade," editorial, *New York Times,* Nov. 5, 2005.

16. Kevin Sheekey on *Inside City Hall,* NY1, Nov. 9, 2005.

17. John Heilemann, "His American Dream," *New York Magazine,* Dec. 3, 2006.

18. Rita Nissan, "Mayor Defends Administration's Decision to Fund All Stars," NY1, Sept. 13, 2006, http://www.ny1.com/content/top_stories/62571/mayor-defends -administration-s-decision-to-fund-all-stars.

19. The New York City IP attempted to interest district attorneys in Manhattan, Staten Island, the Bronx, and Queens in investigating the massive fraud, to no avail.

20. New York State Board of Elections Campaign Finance Disclosure Reports, 2008, http://www.elections.ny.gov/CFViewReports.html.

21. Jacqueline Salit on *The Situation Room,* CNN, Jan. 10, 2008, http://premium.edi-tion.cnn.com/TRANSCRIPTS/0801/10/sitroom.02.html.

22. Rick Brand, "Politics & Power: Driving Home a Bloomberg Bid," *New York Newsday,* Jan. 27, 2007.

23. MacKay had formed the Independence Party of America and made himself chairman. In 2009, he attempted to take over the remaining infrastructure of the national Reform Party but wound up mired in an endless legal maze.

24. Unity08 planned to run a cross-ideological independent presidential and vice presidential ticket in 2008, but the effort foundered for financial and political reasons. It was reconstituted as Americans Elect in 2011.

25. Michael Bloomberg, "I'm Not Running for President, but . . . ," *New York Times,* Feb. 28, 2008.

26. By 2008, the Committee for a Unified Independent Party was also known by the name of its website, IndependentVoting.org.

27. Omar H. Ali, *In the Balance of Power: Independent Black Politics and Third-Party Movements in the United States* (Athens: Ohio University Press, 2008), 2.

28. Michael Barbaro, "In Reversal, Mayor Now Woos Political Parties," *New York Times*, Feb. 19, 2009.

29. In 2009, unbeknownst to the city party, Bloomberg donated $1.1 million to MacKay's state party account, which in 2011 became the catalyst for a criminal trial in which a Republican operative, John Haggerty, was convicted of stealing most of the money for personal use. The state party's role in the affair was never fully accounted for at the trial.

30. Citizens Union, *2010 City Charter Revision Recommendations: Increasing Avenues for Governing and Elections in New York City*, press release, June 30, 2010, http://www.citizensunion.org/www/cu/site/hosting/Reports/0610CU_Charter_Revision_Report&Recommendations.pdf.

31. "Redoing the City Charter," editorial, *New York Times*, April 10, 2010.

32. "New York-Election Results," *New York Times*, Nov. 2010, http://elections.nytimes.com/2010/results/new-york?scp=1&sq=%22New%20York%20Election%20Results%22&st=cse.

CHAPTER EIGHT

1. *CNN=Politics: Special Report*, Host: Campbell Brown, CNN, Feb. 5, 2010.

2. FairVote.org, http://www.fairvote.org/congressional-primaries-open-closed-semi-closed-and-top-two (accessed Nov. 29, 2011).

3. Jeff Zeleny and Megan Thee-Brenan, "New Poll Finds a Deep Distrust of Government," *New York Times*, Oct. 25, 2011, http://www.nytimes.com/2011/10/26/us/politics/poll-finds-anxiety-on-the-economy-fuels-volatility-in-the-2012-race.html?_r=1.

4. Mickey Edwards, "How to Turn Republicans and Democrats into Americans," *Atlantic*, July/August 2011.

5. Shane Goldmacher, "Schwarzenegger Taps Abel Maldonado for Lieutenant Governor," *Los Angeles Times*, Nov. 24, 2009.

6. IndependentVoice.Org is the California affiliate of IndependentVoting.org.

7. *California Democratic Party v. Jones*, 530 U.S. 567 (2000).

8. The Progressive Era was a period of social activism and reform that flourished from the 1890s to the 1920s. Among the political reforms that took root at that time were party primaries (replacing direct party bossism in the selection of candidates), citizens' initiative and referendum, and recall.

9. *California Democratic Party v. Jones*, 984 F. Supp. 1288, 1301 (E.D.C.A. 1997).

10. *California Democratic Party v. Jones*, 169 F.3d 646 (9th Cir. 1999).

11. *California Democratic Party v. Jones*, 530 U.S. at 574-575.

12. *California Democratic Party v. Jones*, 530 U.S. at 595.

13. Washington State Secretary of State, http://vote.wa.gov/Elections/Results/Measures.aspx?e=a3501711-c318-45f4-8a03-1d926ac839b7.

14. The parties in Washington went to court to challenge Top Two. However, in 2008, the Supreme Court ruled in *Washington State Grange v. Washington State Republican Party* [552 U.S. 442 (2008)] that the Top Two primary was constitutionally permissible. Justice Clarence Thomas wrote the majority opinion. Scalia dissented.

15. California Secretary of State, http://www.sos.ca.gov/elections/sov/2004_general/formatted_ballot_measures_detail.pdf.

16. California Secretary of State, http://www.sos.ca.gov/elections/elections_u.htm.

17. "Proposition 14: Create Real Competition," editorial, *San Francisco Chronicle,* Aug. 25, 2010.

18. "Ralph Nader Warns Californians: Vote NO on Proposition 14—Stop the 'Top Two' Tyranny," news release from *Free and Equal,* posted by J. Kohn, June 2, 2010, http://www.freeandequal.org.

19. Harry Kresky, "Should State Adopt an Open Primary? Yes. It Would Help Third Parties Thrive Where They Now Flunk," *Sacramento Bee,* March 28, 2010.

20. Ibid.

21. Jesse McKinley, "Calif. Voting Change Could Signal Big Political Shift," *New York Times,* June 9, 2010.

22. See IndependentVoice.Org website for full press statement video by Joyce Dattner.

23. Patrick McGreevy and Jack Dolan, "Prop. 14 Promises Political Sea Change," *Los Angeles Times,* June 10, 2010.

24. In late 2010, two lawsuits were filed by third-party activists, *Field v. Bowen* [2010 Cal. LEXIS 12902 (Sup. Ct. Cal. 2010)] and *Chamness v. Bowen* [2011 U.S. Dist. LEXIS 94876 (C.D. Cal. 2011)], that alleged two aspects of California's Top Two primary system are unconstitutional and should therefore prevent Proposition 14 from being enacted. The two details attacked in these suits were the ban on counting write-in votes and the ban on the use of a party identifier for candidates of unqualified parties. These suits were unsuccessful.

    In November 2011, the Peace & Freedom Party and the Libertarian Party of California, along with the Green Party of Alameda County, filed a lawsuit in Superior Court in Alameda County, *Rubin v. Bowen* [RG 11-605301 (Superior Court of Cal., Alameda County 2011)], that challenged the constitutionality of Top Two primaries altogether. The complaint states that Proposition 14 violates the rights of voters to vote freely in November and violates the associational rights of political parties and their candidates.

25. *The Dylan Ratigan Show,* MSNBC, July 30, 2010.

26. *20th Public Policy Survey,* Boise State University Public Policy Center, 2011.

27. John Miller, "U.S. District Court Judge: Independents' Lawyers May Intervene in Idaho Primary Lawsuit," *IdahoStatesman,* Aug. 20, 2008, http://www.idaho statesman.com/2008/08/20/476538/us-district-court-judge-independents .html#storylink=misearch.

28. *Idaho Republican Party v. Ysursa,* 765 F. Supp. 2d 1266, 1275 (D. Idaho 2011).

29. The Democratic Party opened its primaries to independents.

30. *Greenville County Republican Party Executive Committee v. South Carolina,* 2011U.S. Dist. LEXIS 35967, p. 28 (D.S.C. March 30, 2011).

31. Ted Downing on *The Buckmaster Show,* Oct. 5, 2011, http://www.buckmaster show.com/2011/10/05/buckmaster-show-1052011-radical-overhaul-of-arizona -primary-system-proposed/.

32. Francis Fukuyama, *The Origins of Political Order: From Prehuman Times to the French Revolution* (New York: Farrar, Straus & Giroux, 2011), 16.

CHAPTER NINE

1. W.E.B. Du Bois, *An ABC of Color: Selections Chosen by the Author from over a Half Century of His Writings* (New York: International Publishers, 1969), 124–25.

2. "The Black Agenda/The Gary Declaration: Black Politics at the Crossroads," National Black Political Convention, 1972, BlackPast.org, http://blackpast.org /?q=primary/gary-declaration-national-black-political-convention-1972.

3. Ronald W. Walters, *Black Presidential Politics in America: A Strategic Approach* (Albany: State University of New York, 1988), 87.

4. For detailed accounts, see Omar H. Ali, *In the Balance of Power: Independent Black Politics and Third-Party Movements in the United States* (Athens: Ohio University Press, 2008).

5. Lenora Fulani, Ph.D., "Bringing Ralph Nader to Harlem," *Souls: A Critical Journal of Black Politics, Culture and Society,* 7:2, 2005, 40.

6. A single-member district system results in sending one officeholder to a legislative body from a distinct geographical area. During and after Reconstruction, many majority white jurisdictions switched to at-large and multimember election systems in order to ensure sending whites-only delegations to their state legislatures and town councils.

   In 1965 Congress passed the Voting Rights Act, and civil rights activists began pushing for the creation of "minority-majority" single-member districts, which would allow for the election of African American legislators. However, the Supreme Court ruled in 1980 that multimember districts were not by definition discriminatory, and minorities must prove, on a case-by-case basis, that such districts were intentionally implemented to diminish their vote. Congress responded by enacting the Voting Rights Act of 1982 that guaranteed judicial relief from election structures that diluted the voting power of minorities.

   After 1982 state legislatures accelerated the creation of minority-majority, single-member districts that would comply with both the constitutional requirement that districts have equal numbers of citizens and the antivote dilution muscle of the Voting Rights Act. New minority-majority, single-member districts led to a spike in office holding among African Americans and other minorities.

7. Rev. Al Sharpton, The National Alliance, April 19, 1990.

8. New York State Board of Elections, General Election Vote, Nov. 6, 1990.

9. Alison Mitchell, "Sharpton's Headache: To Get Out the Vote," *New York Times,* Sept. 9, 1992.

10. James S. Jackson, "National Black Election Panel Study, 1984 and 1988," conducted by University of Michigan, Research Center for Group Dynamics, ICPSR ed., Ann Arbor, MI: Inter-university Consortium for Political and Social Research, producer and distributor, 1993. (In 1985 James Jackson presented his findings to a Chicago meeting of independent black leaders, Lenora Fulani and the New Alliance Party's 1984 presidential candidate, Dennis Serrette, among them.)

11. http://www.jointcenter.org/sites/default/files/upload/research/files/2000-NOP -Politics%20-%2024%20pages.pdf.

12. From a letter by Loretta King, acting Assistant Attorney General of the Civil Rights Division of the U.S. Department of Justice, invalidating a vote by the citizens of Kinston, NC for nonpartisan elections (August 17, 2009).

13. Whether this reconsideration and ultimate reversal was a function of new facts "on the ground" or DOJ's concern that litigation in response to its initial overturn of the Kinston election results could have led to the federal court finding Section 5 of the Voting Rights Act unconstitutional, is unclear.

14. Ali, *In the Balance of Power,* 111–112.

15. See Ali, *In the Balance of Power,* for a thorough historical treatment of this issue.

CHAPTER TEN

1. If not for independents voting in the open primaries, Hillary Clinton would have won the Democratic Party nomination and surpassed Obama's primary totals by 373,910 votes. (Source: Election Center 2008 Exit Poll data, CNN.com.)

2. Edison Media Research, 2008 Exit Poll Data.

3. John Heilemann, "The New Politics: Barack Obama: Party of One," *New York Magazine,* Jan.19, 2009, http://nymag.com/news/features/all-new/53380/.

4. Neil King Jr., "Antsy Voters Look for a Third Way," *Wall Street Journal,* Nov. 26, 2011, http://online.wsj.com/article/SB10001424052970203710704577054501776 975774.html.

5. Albert Hunt, "Third-Party Chestnut Won't Fix Broken U.S. Politics," Bloomberg News, July 31, 2011, http://www.bloomberg.com/news/2011-07-31/third-party -chestnut-won-t-fix-broken-u-s-politics-albert-hunt.html.

6. Thomas L. Friedman, "Make Way for the Radical Center," *New York Times,* July 23, 2011, http://www.nytimes.com/2011/07/24/opinion/sunday/24friedman.html ?_r=1&scp=1&sq=%22Tom%20Friedman%22%20%22Americans%20Elect%22 &st=cse&gwh=48B364D4A4D6365E991FBEA3378DA9DE.

7. Fred Newman and Jackie Salit, *Talk/Talk: Making (Non)Sense of an Irrational World* (New York: CUIP/IndependentVoting.org, 2010), 59–65.

8. George Washington's Farewell Address to the People of the United States, Published in *The Independent Chronicle—September 26, 1796,* http://www.early america.com/earlyamerica/milestones/farewell/.

BIBLIOGRAPHY

Ali, Omar H. *In the Balance of Power: Independent Black Politics and Third-Party Movements in the United States.* Athens: Ohio University Press, 2008.

Ali, Omar H. *In the Lion's Mouth: Black Populism in the New South, 1886-1900.* Jackson: University of Mississippi Press, 2010.

Amato, Theresa. *Grand Illusion: The Myth of Voter Choice in a Two-Party Tyranny.* New York: New Press, 2009.

Barry, Francis S. *The Scandal of Reform: The Grand Failures of New York's Political Crusaders and the Death of Nonpartisanship.* New Brunswick, NJ: Rutgers University Press, 2009.

Black, Gordon S., and Benjamin D. Black. *The Politics of American Discontent: How a New Party Can Make Democracy Work Again.* New York: John Wiley & Sons, 1994.

Brownstein, Ronald. *The Second Civil War: How Extreme Partisanship Has Paralyzed Washington and Polarized America.* New York: Penguin Press, 2007.

Clinton, Bill. *My Life.* New York: Alfred A. Knopf, 2004.

Committee for a Unified Independent Party, Inc. *Can Independents Reform America?* DVD. New York: CUIP, 2011.

Committee for a Unified Independent Party, Inc. *How the Independent Movement Went Left by Going Right: The Untold Story of the Movement that Elected America's First Independent President.* DVD. New York: CUIP, 2009.

Du Bois, W.E.B. *An ABC of Color: Selections Chosen by the Author from over a Half Century of His Writings.* New York: International Publishers, 1969.

Du Bois, W. E. B. *The Souls of Black Folk.* New York: Dover Publications, 1994.

Fukuyama, Francis. "The End of History?" *National Interest.* Summer 1989.

Fukuyama, Francis. *The End of History and the Last Man.* New York: Free Press, 1992.

Fukuyama, Francis. *The Origins of Political Order: From Prehuman Times to the French Revolution.* New York: Farrar, Straus & Giroux, 2011.

Fulani, Lenora. *The Making of a Fringe Candidate 1992.* New York: Castillo International, 1992.

Gergen, Kenneth J. *The Saturated Self: Dilemmas of Identity in Contemporary Life.* New York: Basic, 2000.

Greider, William. *One World, Ready or Not: The Manic Logic of Global Capitalism.* New York: Simon & Schuster, 1997.

Halperin, Mark, and John Heilemann. *Game Change: Obama and the Clintons, McCain and Palin, and the Race of a Lifetime.* New York: Harper, 2010.

Hofstadter, Richard. *The Age of Reform: From Bryan to F. D. R.* New York: Knopf, 1955.

Huffington, Arianna. *Third World America: How Our Politicians Are Abandoning the Middle Class and Betraying the American Dream.* New York: Broadway Paperbacks, 2011.

Karp, Walter. *Indispensable Enemies: The Politics of Misrule in America.* New York: Franklin Square Press, 1993.

Kopkind, Andrew, ed. Joann Wypijewski. *The Thirty Years' Wars: Dispatches and Diversions of a Radical Journalist, 1965-1994.* London: Verso Books, 1995.

Menand, Louis. *The Metaphysical Club.* New York: Farrar, Straus & Giroux, 2001.

Morgenson, Gretchen, and Joshua Rosner. *Reckles$ Endangerment: How Outsized Ambition, Greed, and Corruption Led to Economic Armageddon.* New York: Times Books/ Henry Holt, 2011.

Nader, Ralph. *The Good Fight: Declare Your Independence and Close the Democracy Gap.* New York: Regan Books, 2004.

"The National Black Political Agenda," in *The Black Power Movement, Part 1: Amiri Baraka from Black Arts to Black Radicalism,* ed. Komozi Woodard, Randolph Boehm, Daniel Lewis. Bethesda, Maryland: University Publications of America, 2000, microfilm, reel 3. See http://faculty.washington.edu/qtaylor/documents_us /gary_declaration.htm. (accessed Nov. 30, 2011).

Newman, Fred. "The Performance of Revolution (More Thoughts on the Postmodernization of Marxism)." In *Postmodern Psychologies, Societal Practice and Political Life,* ed. Lois Holzman and John Morss, 165-176. New York: Routledge, 2000.

Newman, Fred, and Lois Holzman. *The End of Knowing: A New Developmental Way of Learning.* London: Routledge, 1997.

Newman, Fred, and Jackie Salit. *Talk/Talk: Making (Non) Sense of an Irrational World.* New York: CUIP/IndependentVoting.org, 2010.

Perot, Ross. "Foreword," in *Preparing Our Country for the 21st Century: The Official Transcript of the United We Stand America Conference.* New York: HarperPerennial, 1995.

Posner, Gerald L. *Citizen Perot: His Life and Times.* New York: Random House, 1996.

Ramo, Joshua Cooper. *The Age of the Unthinkable: Why the New World Disorder Constantly Surprises Us and What to Do About It.* New York: Back Bay Books, 2010.

Rapoport, Ronald B., and Walter J. Stone. *Three's a Crowd: The Dynamic of Third Parties, Ross Perot, and Republican Resurgence.* Ann Arbor: The University of Michigan Press, 2005.

Schoen, Douglas E. *Declaring Independence: The Beginning of the End of the Two-Party System.* New York: Random House, 2008.

Schoen, Douglas E. *The Political Fix: Changing the Game of American Democracy, From the Grass Roots to the White House.* New York: Times Books/Henry Holt, 2010.

Sharpton, Al, with Hunter, Karen. *Al on America.* New York: Dafina Books, 2002.

Sifry, Micah L. *Spoiling for a Fight: Third Party Politics in America.* New York: Routledge, 2002.

Tomasky, Michael. *Hillary's Turn: Inside Her Improbable, Victorious Senate Campaign.* New York: Free Press, 2001.

Toynbee, Arnold J. *A Study of History: Abridgment of Volumes I-VI by D.C. Somervell.* Oxford, England: Oxford University Press, 1946.

Walters, Ronald W. *Black Presidential Politics in America: A Strategic Approach.* Albany: State University of New York, 1988.

Washington, George. *Farewell Address to the People of the United States (1796),* http://www.access.gpo.gov/congress/senate/farewell/sd106-21.pdf (accessed Nov. 30, 2011).

Wood, Gordon S. *The Idea of America: Reflections on the Birth of the United States.* New York: Penguin Press, 2011.

INDEX